Bizarre Space

A KID'S GUIDE TO OUR STRANGE,
UNUSUAL UNIVERSE

Bizarre Space

JENN DLUGOS AND CHARLIE HATTON

PRUFROCK PRESS INC.
WACO, TEXAS

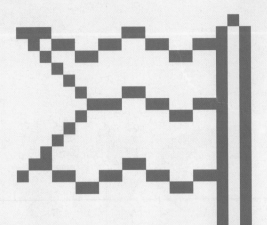

Names: Dlugos, Jenn, author. | Hatton, Charlie, author.
Title: Bizarre space : a kid's guide to our strange, unusual universe / by
    Jenn Dlugos and Charlie Hatton.
Description: Waco, Texas : Prufrock Press, Inc., [2018] | Audience: Age 9-12. |
    Includes bibliographical references.
Identifiers: LCCN 2017030662 (print) | LCCN 2017037309 (ebook) | ISBN
    9781618216908 (pdf) | ISBN 9781618216892 (pbk.)
Subjects: LCSH: Astronomy--Juvenile literature. | Cosmology--Juvenile literature.
Classification: LCC QB46 (ebook) | LCC QB46 .D58 2018 (print) | DDC 523--dc23
LC record available at https://lccn.loc.gov/2017030662

Edited by Stephanie McCauley

Cover and layout design by Allegra Denbo

ISBN-13: 978-1-61821-689-2

Prufrock Press Inc.
P.O. Box 8813
Waco, TX 76714-8813
Phone: (800) 998-2208
Fax: (800) 240-0333
http://www.prufrock.com

TABLE OF CONTENTS

INTRODUCTION

> Space is big. Really big. You just won't believe
> how vastly hugely mind-bogglingly big it is.
>
> —Douglas Adams, *The Hitchhiker's Guide to the Galaxy*

Those words were true when author Douglas Adams wrote them back in the 1970s. Since then, space has only gotten bigger—literally, because the universe is constantly expanding, and also practically, because new telescopes, space probes, and computers let us see deeper into space than ever before. If the bigness of space boggled minds 40 years ago, it's super-duper, doubly boggling now.

As huge as space is, we learn more about it every day. New discoveries are made about stars, planets, galaxies, black holes, and other cosmic mysteries, using equipment all over the Earth and beyond. From observatories atop Maunakea in Hawaii, to telescope arrays in the Chilean desert, to space probes orbiting (and landing on) exotic planets and asteroids, scientists are constantly collecting and analyzing information about the universe around us.

But professional astronomers aren't the only ones exploring space. Amateur scientists can make exciting new discoveries, too. In recent years, weekend stargazers have found new planets, stars, galaxies, and even an asteroid smacking into Jupiter! Group efforts in "citizen science" encourage anyone to scan data to look for planets, classify galaxies, or monitor the sun's behavior. If you have the interest, you could help to make the next big find!

In the meantime, read on to learn about what we currently know—or think we know—about space. Not everything in this book will turn out to be the "final word." No one's ever visited another galaxy or jumped into a black hole, so it's impossible to know for certain how they behave. What you'll find here are science's current theories—explanations that agree with all of the information collected so far. But tomorrow, a new space mission might go farther, or a bizarre new star might be found, and theories may change to fit the new information.

The more we learn, the better our theories become. We know more about Mars, for example, than about the star system Alpha Centauri, because we've studied Mars in more detail. Maybe someday we'll send spacecraft to Alpha Centauri, and stars and galaxies beyond, to unpack more secrets of the distant universe. There's always more to learn, you see. Space is *big*.

Log in to Spacebook!

Have you ever wondered what your favorite planets, moons, and other space objects would write on their social media profiles?

Probably not, because that's a really weird thing to wonder. But we wondered that, so at the beginning of every chapter, take a sneak peek at Spacebook, the hottest social media site in the universe!

(Just don't let Jupiter post a selfie. He's a total pixel hog.)

SECTION 1
The Innies

No, we're not talking about belly buttons. We're talking about planets! Specifically, the planets on the sunnier side of the asteroid belt. Mercury, Venus, Earth, and Mars are terrestrial planets (like the word *terrain*) because they are rocky. These "innies" have a lot in common but also have some incredible—and incredibly bizarre—differences that make each planet one of a kind.

—Urbain Le Verrier

Bizarre Space Trivia

French mathematician Urbain Le Verrier (1811–1877) tried to come up with an explanation for Mercury's unusual orbit. What was his hypothesis?

a. Mercury's orbit went directly through the sun.

b. A planet named Vulcan interfered with Mercury's orbit.

c. A star in our solar system named Uhura tugged on Mercury.

— Find out the answer at the end of the section (p. 35)! —

Mercury

+ **Current Mood:** Hot under the collar

+ **Best Frenemy:** The sun

+ **Wish List:** Sunscreen (SPF 500,000), wrinkle cream, dancing lessons

Timeline: 4.6 billion years ago–now

| 14 Billion Years Ago | | 4.6 Billion Years Ago | Today |

Birth of the Universe

Mercury

A MAGICAL MERCURY TOUR

Sometimes, it's good to be first. Whether you're first in your class, in the first row at the theater, or first in line for ice cream, "first" is a very nice place to be. But if you're a planet, and being first means orbiting the closest to a scorching hot star, it might be better to let someone else in front. Just ask Mercury.

Among our solar system's planets, Mercury is closest to the sun—but it's no picnic being first. In fact, Mercury couldn't host a picnic, even if it wanted to. The surface of Mercury facing the sun reaches 800°F (427°C), or about as hot as fresh lava spewing from a volcano on Earth. At that temperature, the picnic blanket would catch fire, the lemonade would evaporate, and all of the sandwiches would melt. For that matter, so would a picnic basket made of lead. Even ants would avoid a Mercury afternoon picnic. It's just too hot.

But Mercury isn't all blazing sunshine and boiling potato salad. The side of the planet facing away from the sun tends to be cooler. Unfortunately for hopeful picnickers, that side of Mercury can be *1,000 degrees* cooler, all the way down to -290°F. That's far colder than any place on Earth. There's not enough hot cocoa in the galaxy to warm you up after a few minutes at that temperature.

You're as Hot as . . . Ice?

It may seem strange for a planet baking in the sun, but Mercury manages to keep ice frozen at its north and south poles, just as Earth does. On Mercury, this ice lies inside craters near the poles. Even when the craters face the sun, the deep walls inside remain in shadow—and stay cold enough for water to freeze and remain as ice. Scientists believe that ice in some of the craters may still be building up today.

Wherever on Mercury a brave (and hopefully fireproof) explorer might land, the conditions aren't likely to change quickly. Mercury, like all planets in our solar system, spins on its axis, like a twirling top or a basketball spinning on a Harlem Globetrotter's finger. This spinning slowly turns the sunny side of the planet away into darkness and turns the side facing away from the sun into the light. One full spin from light to dark to light—or dark to light to dark, if you're on vampire time—is a "solar day." On Earth, a solar day lasts roughly 24 hours.

(The exact length of a day can be a little longer or shorter, depending on the time of year, phase of the moon, and other factors. Or it can seem *much* longer, if your uncle is telling that same boring story of his, *again*.)

But Mercury spins on its axis much more slowly than Earth. In fact, Mercury spins so slowly, a solar day there lasts 176 Earth days.

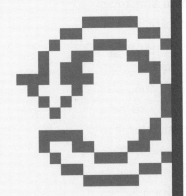

Spin Again, Friend

Mercury's strange rate of spin is unusual, but it's possible that the planet wasn't always such an oddball dancer. Mercury may have behaved more predictably until about 4 billion years ago, when scientists believe an asteroid roughly the size of Rhode Island smacked into the young planet. This violent impact may have created the Caloris Basin, Mercury's largest crater, and set Mercury spinning in the opposite direction, leading to the unruly rotation we see today.

—Mercury passing directly between the sun and Earth. The images of Mercury's journey across the sun were taken in a wavelength of extreme ultraviolet light.

—Light spectrum

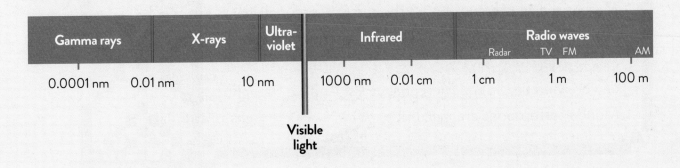

Gamma rays		X-rays	Ultra-violet	Infrared		Radio waves		
						Radar	TV FM	AM
0.0001 nm	0.01 nm		10 nm	1000 nm	0.01 cm	1 cm	1 m	100 m

Visible light

Such a long day might sound great for people who like fun in the sun—2,112 hours of sunshine, every day!—but it's still 800 degrees outside, and the nights last just as long. Mercury isn't quite the summer getaway spot you might hope for.

Apart from the extreme temperatures and strange spins, you might expect Mercury to be a quiet, burnt little rock. It's nearly 3 times closer to the sun than we are on Earth, after all, and that's a lot of heat to deal with. If you leave a bag of popcorn in the microwave just a few minutes too long, the popcorn burns into a black, smoking crisp. Mercury's been baking in the sun since the planets formed 4.6 billion years ago. What could possibly still be happening there?

Actually, quite a bit. Despite the close-up sunbathing, Mercury's iron core is slowly cooling down. As the core cools, it also shrinks, and the outer layers of the planet shrink around it. In fact, scientists estimate that Mercury has contracted in size by 4 miles or more. Apparently, Grandpa isn't the only one who wrinkles and shrinks with age.

What Year Is Today?

On any planet, one trip around the sun is a year—but years aren't always what we're used to on Earth. Because Mercury orbits so close to the sun, it makes the trip around very quickly. Not only is Mercury's year shorter than an Earth year, but a Mercurial year is also shorter than a Mercurial day! Mercury circles the sun (a Mercurial year) every 88 Earth days but makes a full rotation around its axis (a Mercurial day) only every 176 Earth days. So a day on Mercury lasts 2 Mercurial years. And we thought Monday afternoons dragged on!

The most dramatic feature suggesting shrinkage on Mercury is a "great valley" scarring the planet's southern hemisphere. This huge valley is more than 620 miles long, 250 miles wide, and 2 miles deep, making it longer than the Grand Canyon and wider and deeper than Africa's Great Rift Valley. That's a big dent in a rock less than 40% of Earth's size—and shrinking all the time. But it's just another surprise from the solar system's "first" planet, mysterious Mercury.

—Mercury shows signs of aging

How Do We Know What We Know?

Just two NASA missions have provided most of our Mercury knowledge—the Mariner 10 probe, launched in 1973, and 2004's MESSENGER probe, which mapped Mercury's entire surface and was crashed on purpose onto the planet in 2015. NASA's Project Mercury, on the other hand, had nothing to do with the sun-soaked planet. It consisted of space missions in the late 1950s and early 1960s that led to John Glenn becoming one of the first humans to orbit the Earth.

Venus

+ **Current Mood:** Full o' love

+ **Favorite TV Show:** *Curb Your Venus-thusiasm*

+ **Favorite Song:** "(You Make Me Feel) Like a Natural Woman"

Timeline: 4.6 billion years ago—now

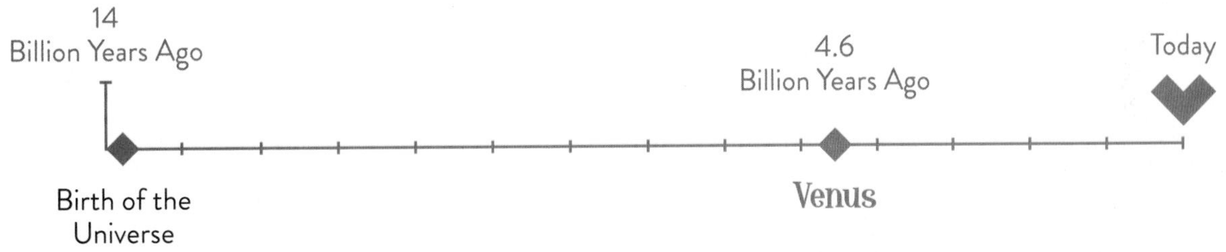

| 14 Billion Years Ago | 4.6 Billion Years Ago | Today |

Birth of the Universe

Venus

WON'T YOU BE MY VENUSTINE?

Star light, star bright, the brightest "star" you see tonight . . . may not even be a star. Venus is the third brightest object in our sky (after the sun and the moon), and it is the only female-named planet in our solar system. Venus was the Roman goddess of love and beauty, which is why it's no great surprise that she looks "simply *gorgeous*, darling" in our sky.

Venus is Earth's closest planetary neighbor, and it also orbits a bit closer to the sun than we do. But despite its beauty and extra sun, Venus is certainly not going to replace Aruba as a dream vacation spot anytime soon. For one, Venus is a lot hotter. In fact, it's the hottest planet in our solar system—even hotter

11

than Mercury! Temperatures on Venus exceed 860°F (460°C) on the surface, which is quite a bit warmer than Aruba, even during a heat wave.

This extreme heat is mostly due to Venus's thick atmosphere, which is made up primarily of carbon dioxide and has an atmospheric pressure that is 100 times greater than Earth's. Carbon dioxide is a greenhouse gas, meaning it traps the heat of the sun. Even if you survived your tropical Venus vacation (Spoiler alert: You won't—not in a Bermuda shirt and flip-flops, anyway), you probably won't even see much of the sun because of the thick sulfur clouds in the atmosphere.

(Seriously, go to Aruba. They have dolphins there.)

Heavy Metal Jack Frost

On Earth, the sun's heat causes liquid water to evaporate into water vapor. On Venus, it gets so hot that metallic minerals on the planet's surface evaporate, forming a metal mist in the air. At higher elevations, this mist cools, and it falls as metal snow. If Venus weren't scary enough, there is always a possibility you could run into Frosty the Metalman thumpity-thump-thumping down the street.

Venus *really* wants to make its presence known. It's already one of the brightest objects in our sky. But now, it's waving at us.

Japan's Akatsuki Venus Climate Orbiter captured a stunning picture of a massive bow-shaped wave in Venus's atmosphere—more than 6,200 miles (9,978 kilometers) long. The wave lasted 4 days, and scientists were quite confused by it. The wave was rather stationary, which is odd because Venus's atmosphere has a super-rotation. Basically, Venus rotates very slowly—a day on Venus is about 243 Earth days. But the atmosphere on Venus rotates much faster—one rotation takes about 4 Earth days. This super-rotation is one of the biggest mysteries of Venus, because scientists still do not exactly know why it happens.

So what was this giant wave in Venus's atmosphere? It could have been a gravity wave, which occurs when winds move over certain planetary features, like mountains. The wind pushes air upward into the atmosphere, causing a wave-like effect. This wave was found above a large mountainous region called

—Transit of Venus across the sun observed from the International Space Station on June 5, 2012

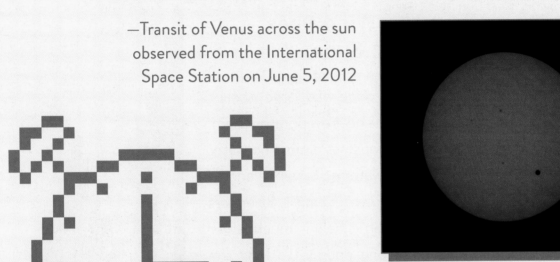

Riding on the VTA
(Venus Transit Authority)

From Earth, we can occasionally see Venus in transit across the sun. It looks like a little black ball moving across the sun's surface. The bad news? Although two transits of Venus occurred recently—in 2004 and 2012—the next won't occur until 2117. We only see this transit when Venus, Earth, and the sun are lined up just right. This doesn't happen often because Venus's orbit is shorter and tilted at a different angle than Earth's. During that 105-year window, we'll just keep missing each other. Maybe one of us should try texting?

Aphrodite Terra (appropriately named for Venus, as Aphrodite is the Greek goddess of love). This possible explanation raises many more questions about Venus's atmosphere, and more research needs to be done. In the meantime, we suppose that when Venus waves at us, it's only polite to wave back.

When Even the Wind Does the Electric Slide

Scientists think that Venus once had large oceans much like Earth's, but the extreme heat evaporated them. However, the atmosphere of Venus has almost no water vapor, so exactly where did this water go? Every planet is believed to have an electric field surrounding it. Scientists recently found that Venus's electric field is much larger than Earth's and could be strong enough to fling the atoms that make up water into space. Simply put, as water evaporated, Venus could have flung its oceans into space with this "electric wind."

We have four distinct seasons on Earth, primarily due to Earth's 23-degree tilt on its axis. Venus has a 177-degree tilt. Because 180 degrees is straight up and down, Venus is practically standing on its head. (Maybe it really digs yoga. It seems like a natural for the downward-facing planet pose.) It's also unusual because it rotates backward (called *retrograde rotation*). Because it rotates rather slowly, Venus doesn't have seasons in the way we experience them on Earth, nor does it have day-to-night temperature changes every 24 hours. So, if you're waiting for the weather on Venus to become more livable, don't hold your breath.

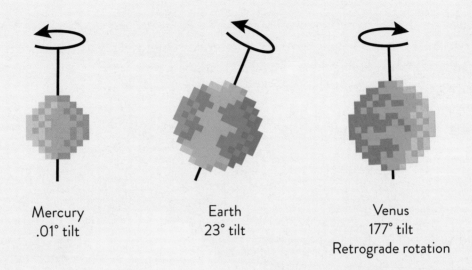

Mercury
.01° tilt

Earth
23° tilt

Venus
177° tilt
Retrograde rotation

Was Venus's climate always so inhospitable to life? NASA's Goddard Institute for Space Studies (GISS) recently created a climate model of ancient Venus using modeling software that predicts climate changes on Earth. The model found that not only was it possible for ancient Venus to be habitable, it's also possible that the climate could have been a few degrees cooler than Earth's climate. If this is true, then what caused Venus to be so full of hot air? One possible theory is that an early collision with a large planetary object could have created enough heat to change Venus's atmosphere. But we really don't know for sure. Until we do, we humans will just keep off our hot-tempered planetary neighbor's charbroiled lawn.

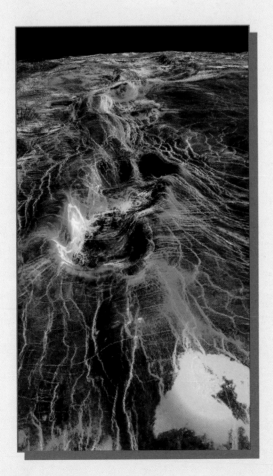

—This perspective view of Venus, generated by a computer and color-coded, shows part of the lowland plains. The circular depressions are called *coronae*.

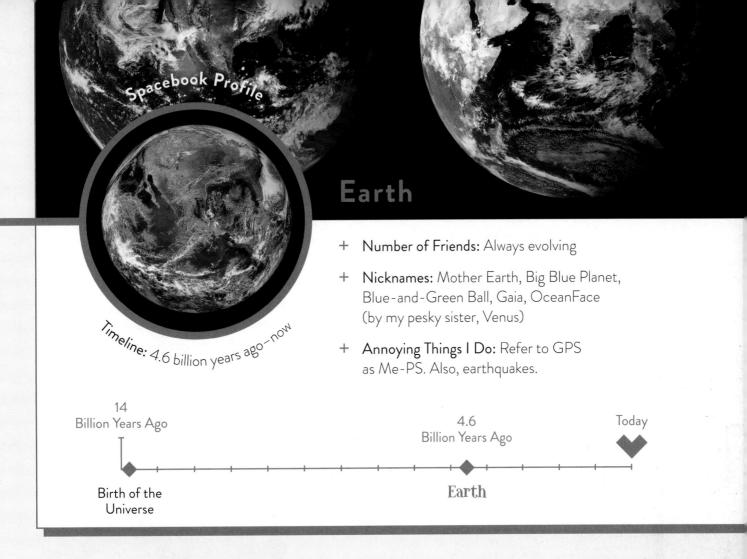

Earth

+ **Number of Friends:** Always evolving

+ **Nicknames:** Mother Earth, Big Blue Planet, Blue-and-Green Ball, Gaia, OceanFace (by my pesky sister, Venus)

+ **Annoying Things I Do:** Refer to GPS as Me-PS. Also, earthquakes.

Timeline: 4.6 billion years ago–now

14 Billion Years Ago	4.6 Billion Years Ago	Today
Birth of the Universe	Earth	

OUR (H)EARTH AND HOME

It's good to be home sweet home, at least in the planetary sense. For those of us who live, breathe, and poop on this planet, there is nowhere else we should (or should *want*) to be. After all, our nearest planetary neighbors are not exactly accommodating to our lifestyle. (We're looking at you, Mars and Venus.) But how did Earth become the biggest party in the solar system with millions of species creeping, crawling, and cha-cha-ing across its surface?

Lucky for us, Earth falls into something called the *habitable zone*, which means it's close enough to the sun to keep us toasty, but far enough away that the sun's heat doesn't completely evaporate our surface water. The habitable zone is sometimes called the *Goldilocks zone*—it's neither too far from nor too close to its star; it's just right. When scientists look for Earth-like planets, they look for planets that fall into this zone.

But "being in the zone" only gets us so far. Earth's atmosphere is rich in oxygen, which almost all of us down here need to survive. (We say "almost all" because there are some freaky organisms called *obligate anaerobes* that die in the presence of oxygen. When you have the biggest party in the solar system, a few weirdos are bound to show up.) The Earth also has many geological processes, some deep underneath its surface, that help make life possible. The answer to "Why can Earth support life?" is quite complex, but it also makes our little blue-and-green ball one of a kind.

What's in a Name?

Earth is the only planet in our solar system that's not named after a god. It's derived from the German word *erde* and the English word *ertha*, which both mean "ground." Even though Earth is not named after a god, the Greek goddess Gaea, or Mother Gaea, is known as *Mother Earth*.

—Earth has a blue halo when seen from space because of the gases in the atmosphere

Don't Have Enough Time in Your Day?

Well, good news! Earth's rotation is slowing down due to a phenomenon called *tidal friction*. Basically, the moon's gravitational pull is causing the Earth to lose some of its "groove," specifically the momentum of its rotation. This doesn't mean you can procrastinate on your homework tonight, however. Scientists estimate that it'll be 200 million years before we have a full 25-hour day.

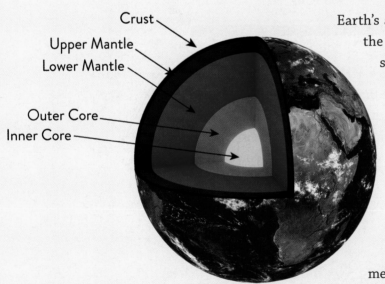

Crust
Upper Mantle
Lower Mantle
Outer Core
Inner Core

Earth's atmosphere protects us from the extreme temperatures of space, but it doesn't shield us effectively from the sun's radiation and its powerful solar weather. Solar winds can destroy an atmosphere (just wait until you see what they did to Mars), so why does Earth's atmosphere survive?

The answer lies in a hard metal ball surrounded by a molten metal core in the center of our planet. This molten core is made of liquid iron and nickel, and it's a big hot mess. The temperature here is as hot as the sun, and it makes geothermal energy possible. Today, the heat from underneath the Earth's crust can be used to make electricity and heat homes. The ancient Romans built magnificent bathhouses powered by natural hot water springs that were heated by geothermal processes.

This liquid outer core is also responsible for the Earth's magnetic field that shields us from the high-dose radiation of the sun. The magnetic field is weaker at the equator than it is at the poles, and it also weakens the farther

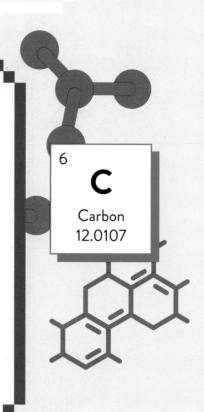

Life is a Cabaret? Try a Carbon-aret!

All organisms on Earth have carbon in their bodies, so having carbon available at the Earth's surface is important to life on this planet. In 2016, scientists from Rice University proposed that this carbon could have originated from a Mercury-sized planet that collided with Earth 4.4 billion years ago. That smaller planet's core was sucked into Earth's own core, and the planet's carbon-rich upper layer became part of Earth's mantle. If this theory is true, then let's give a special thanks to this Mercury-sized planet for doing us a solid (solid carbon, that is).

| 6 |
| C |
| Carbon |
| 12.0107 |

you get from the Earth's surface. If you've ever heard that you are exposed to more radiation on an airplane than on land, it's because the magnetic field is weaker as you rise. This isn't much of a concern to the casual Earth-based traveler, but it is a big concern for astronauts because they experience more radiation the farther they travel from our planet's surface.

Earth's Magnetic Field

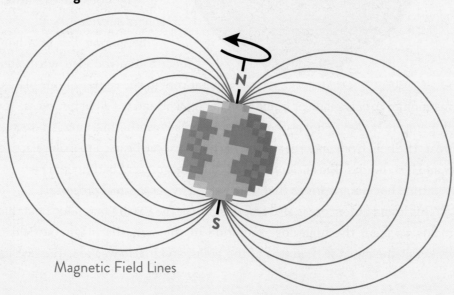

Magnetic Field Lines

Due to our all-season pass to the nightly moon show, we get to see crazy things like blood moons, when the moon appears red because it passed into the Earth's shadow during a lunar eclipse. There is also the supermoon that occurs when a full moon appears during the moon's closest possible distance to Earth. On these nights, the moon looks Hulk-sized in the sky. (Don't worry about going outside to look at it. Current scientific evidence states that super-moons do *not* create super-werewolves.)

When Life Hands You a Lemon, Make Moon-ade?

The moon may look like a bright, beautiful ball in our night sky, but it's shaped more like a lemon, with a big bulge in the middle. This widening of the moon's midsection could have occurred shortly after the moon was formed. The moon was mostly hot liquid rock, and the gravitational pull of the Earth could have created the bulge that makes the moon look like we all feel after Thanksgiving dinner.

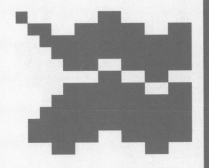

The moon is rather special to humans because it's the first celestial body we stepped foot on other than our own Earth. But what happens when astronauts visit the moon? Do they find that it has all the comforts of a home away from home?

Not exactly. For one, the moon has a very weak atmosphere, and the temperature there can change drastically. During a lunar eclipse, when the moon passes into Earth's shadow, the surface temperature of the moon can drop 500°F in 90 minutes. (Mental note: If you go to the moon, pack long underwear.) At its equator during the day, the moon can reach temperatures of 280°F. (Mental note: Also, pack sunscreen: SPF 800.)

There's also the time change, at least based on what we consider a day. In 1970, Kenneth L. Franklin, who was the chief astronomer at the Hayden Planetarium, designed a watch for future moonwalkers based on one moon day (which is 29.530589 Earth days). One of the watches was gifted to President Richard Nixon.

If you happen to find yourself strolling on the moon, be careful with your footing. The moon only has 17% of the Earth's gravity, which is why moonwalkers appear to bounce as they walk across the moon's surface. The moon also has "moonquakes," which can last a lot longer than earthquakes. Earthquakes last 10 to 30 seconds, while a moonquake can last an hour.

One Giant Leap for Treekind

In 1971, NASA scientist Stuart Roosa boarded the Apollo 14 space mission with seeds from redwood, sycamore, and a few other tree species. The craft orbited the moon 34 times before returning to Earth. The seeds were planted on Earth, to see if the conditions of outer space affected their growth, but most of them grew just as well as their Earth-based counterparts. Roosa passed away in 1994, but his famous "moon trees" still grow all over the world.

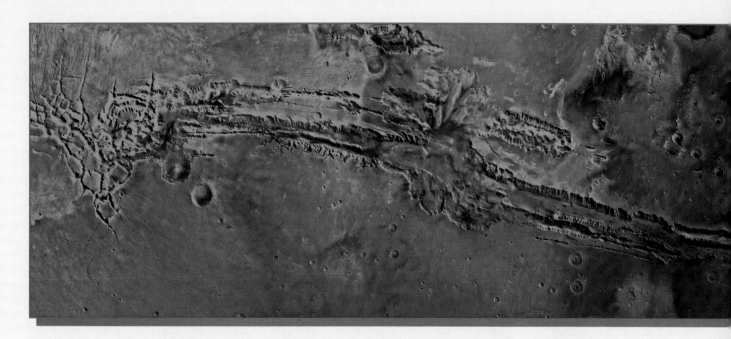

—Valles Marineris is a vast canyon system that runs along the Martian equator. At 4,500 km long, 200 km wide, and 11 km deep, it is 10 times longer, 7 times wider, and 7 times deeper than the Grand Canyon, making it the largest known crevice in the solar system.

—Olympus Mons on Mars

Currently, Mars is orbited by two moons, Deimos and Phobos. And it's a good thing Mars has a "spare" moon, because Phobos is not in good shape. It orbits closer to Mars than any other planet's moon in our solar system, just 3,700 miles from the surface. That's about the distance from Washington, DC, to London, England. But instead of Big Ben and Buckingham Palace on the other side, it's a big looming moon— and looming closer all the time. Mars's gravity pulls Phobos about 6 feet nearer every 100 years, which is also pulling Phobos apart from the stress. Within 30 to 50 million years, the moon will either break into pieces and form a ring around Mars, or crash onto the surface. So, if you visit Mars, be sure to take a good umbrella.

—The moons of Mars: the inner moon Phobos and the outer moon Deimos

More Than One Moon Can Bear

Although Mars may pull Phobos to its final doom, the little moon has already taken a few hard knocks. Phobos's surface is covered in craters formed from impacts with smaller bodies; the largest, Stickney crater, is nearly half the width of the moon! The huge crater gives Phobos the appearance of a giant eyeball, and the impact likely nearly broke the moon apart. Instead, the "eyeball" will one day get a very, *very* close look at the surface of Mars.

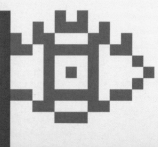

—Phobos's Stickney crater

As close as Mars is to Earth, you might think it's a popular target for scientists to launch space probes and landers. You would be correct. But with all the perils on, above, and around Mars—not to mention that it's still millions of miles away, at best—you might also suspect that some Mars space missions don't go quite as planned. You would be correct again. *Very* correct.

From 1960 through 2016, 53 missions were launched by the USA, Russia/Soviet Union, Japan, European Space Agency (ESA), and India, each with Mars as the target. Of those, 30 (including the first six) failed without completing the mission goals. Finally, NASA's Mariner 4 probe proved "seventh time's a charm" and snapped the first close-up pictures of Mars in 1965. Many of the doomed Mars missions failed during launch or near Earth's orbit. Mars can hardly be blamed for those—but even spacecraft that reached the red planet have had their troubles.

Despite everything—the hostile conditions, the dangers of getting there, and the severe lack of pizza delivery options—some people are determined to travel to Mars. Whether it's the thrill of new discoveries, the challenge of survival, or the awe of stepping onto an alien planet, government and private groups alike hope to send humans to Mars, maybe even by the 2030s.

Soft Landing, Hard Problem

On October 19, 2016, the ESA's Schiaparelli lander approached Mars. Seven miles from the surface, the lander's parachute deployed, slowing the craft from a speed of more than 1,000 miles per hour. Everything went as planned—until a haywire reading led Schiaparelli to calculate that it had already fallen below Mars's surface. The lander released its chute, still more than 2 miles up. Schiaparelli crashed onto the planet, the latest of the Mars mission casualties.

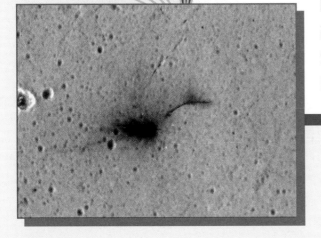

—Schiaparelli impact site on Mars

IS THAT A REAL THING?
Space Disease

By the 1940s, scientists had built rockets that could reach space. They hoped to launch those rockets with people aboard—but no one knew whether it was safe. Scientists and astronauts-to-be worried we couldn't survive in space, even with spacecraft and special suits.

Some thought the low gravity in space might kill a person. Others worried that outside Earth's protective atmosphere, harmful radiation could be instantly fatal. Still others believed that leaving Earth and living in cramped space modules would drive astronauts mad.

Careful research put these fears to rest. Scientists studied radiation in space to determine safe levels of exposure. They also tested animals sent into space—including monkeys, dogs, and mice—and found that low gravity and "space madness" were no problem for space explorers.

Humans soon made the giant leap to space missions, and successful trips into orbit and to the moon. But as some people spent more time in space, it became clear that long-term astronauts do face health risks, including some familiar ones.

Although low levels of gravity and radiation aren't harmful right away, their effects build up over time. After about 6 months in space, low gravity starts to change astronauts' eyesight, hearts, muscles, and bones. Meanwhile, cosmic radiation can damage DNA and impair brain function. So "low gravity disease" and "space madness" actually could develop—but they'll take a while to appear.

—FROM PAGE 3 . . .

—Urbain Le Verrier

Bizarre Space Trivia, Answer

French mathematician Urbain Le Verrier (1811–1877) tried to come up with an explanation for Mercury's unusual orbit. What was his hypothesis?

a. Mercury's orbit went directly through the sun.

b. A planet named Vulcan interfered with Mercury's orbit. (correct)

c. A star in our solar system named Uhura tugged on Mercury.

The Details: Urbain Le Verrier had a big problem with Mercury. It wobbled, and Isaac Newton's theories of gravity didn't adequately explain why. Le Verrier concluded that another planet orbiting even closer to the sun caused this unusual wobble. In 1859, Edmond Lescarbault, a French doctor and astronomy enthusiast, spotted something in his telescope, which he thought was this so-called planet. He contacted Le Verrier about the discovery, and the planet was soon called *Vulcan.* Vulcan-mania swept the globe. Newspapers reported about this new planet, and everyone with a telescope was outside peeping at the sky. But Albert Einstein's theory of relativity eventually explained Mercury's wobble, and the Vulcan theory was debunked. There is no planet Vulcan in our solar system. Sorry, Spock.

(Also, we don't have another star in our solar system named Uhura. She's much too busy on the USS *Enterprise.*)

from the water clouds that float underneath the ammonia clouds. Jupiter's weather patterns have a similar physics to the weather patterns on Earth, so peeking at Jupiter can help us better understand weather on our own blue-and-green ball.

Jupiter is famous for its Great Red Spot, which is a gigantic hurricane-like storm the size of Earth. The storm has been observed on Jupiter for more than 150 years, and the winds reach 400 miles an hour. It's quite a mystery, and scientists are still not exactly sure what causes the spot to be red. However, new evidence suggests that this stubbornly persistent storm may very well heat up the entire planet.

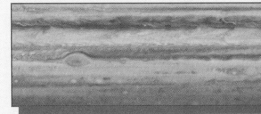

—Jupiter's Great Red Spot

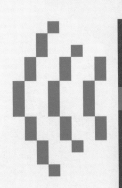

A Big Gassy Neighbor That Blares His Radio

Jupiter has intense radio storms, which can even be heard on radio stations on Earth. Jupiter's magnetic field extends 2 million miles, making it the largest planetary magnetic field in our solar system. When the spacecraft Juno reached the bow shock around Jupiter (the region where solar winds hit Jupiter's magnetic field), it recorded a sonic boom of turbulence. You can hear the sound recorded by Juno by searching "Juno bow shock" on NASA's website (https://www.nasa.gov).

—Ammonia

Earth's atmosphere is mainly heated when heat from the ground is released into the atmosphere. But Jupiter, which is a lot farther from the sun, has a warmer upper atmosphere than scientists can justify simply by solar heating. Some scientists theorize that the Great Red Spot may create turbulent energy waves that smash into each other and heat the upper atmosphere.

The Stripe That Got Away (But Came Back)

In early 2010, amateur astronomers noticed that one of Jupiter's signature dark brown stripes, called the *Southern Equatorial Belt*, had disappeared. In November of that year, the band started to reappear. It tends to disappear every few decades, and it's the only band that shows such a pronounced change. Scientists concluded the 2010 wardrobe change was caused by huge clouds of ammonia ice, which caused the band to have a ghostly white appearance.

July 23, 2009   **Early 2010**

(23.8 million kilometers) from Jupiter. By comparison, Earth's moon only orbits about 238,900 miles away from Earth. The next time someone says "I love you to the moon and back," ask them if those are Earth or Jupiter numbers, because Jupiter is a *lot* farther.

—A basin on Callisto covered in white "scars"

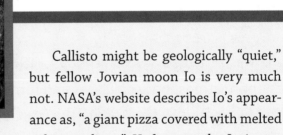

Wanna See My Scars?

Compared to other moons, Callisto seems like a shy wallflower. It's considered geologically "quiet," meaning its surface doesn't get a "facelift" from volcanic eruptions or other processes. Callisto's surface is estimated to be 4 billion years old, the oldest known surface in our solar system. It's also covered in craters that look like white "scars" in photos.

Callisto might be geologically "quiet," but fellow Jovian moon Io is very much not. NASA's website describes Io's appearance as, "a giant pizza covered with melted cheese and splotches of tomato and ripe olives." Unfortunately, Io is not nearly that delicious.

Due to Jupiter's magnetic field, Io basically turns into an electric generator as it rotates. The radiation Io creates is so powerful that it would kill a human instantly. Io is also the most volcanically active spot in our solar system. Jupiter's strong gravitational pull contributes to volcanic eruptions on Io that spew sulfur up to 190 feet (about 58 meters) in the air. That's as tall as Cinderella's castle at Disney World! Being far from the sun, Io's surface temperature is very cold—about -202°F (or -130°C), but its volcanoes reach temperatures up to

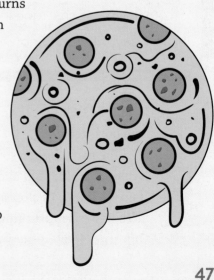

—A view of Io, and a surface view of deposits from a volcano

The Sky Is Falling (No, Really)

If Io wasn't already weird enough, scientists found that its entire atmosphere collapses and turns to frost for 2 hours during its 42-hour orbit. This happens when Io passes into Jupiter's shadow. It must be quite a sight to wake up and find the entire atmosphere frozen on your front lawn. (If that doesn't cause schools to close for a snow day, we don't know what will.)

3,000°F (1,649°C). It's rare to find a moon where Heat Miser and Snow Miser can both get along.

The name *Europa* sounds like a beautiful paradise, and it just might be for scientists. Although about 25% of Europa's surface is made up of chaos terrain—a bunch of slopes, plains, and ridges jumbled together due to geologic activity—scientists think there's a possibility for life in the giant ocean on our solar system, Saturn is a strong source of gravity, which allows it to maintain these massive rings.

Saturn's rings may even be larger than scientists think. In 2008, NASA researchers discovered a ring around Saturn that had never been seen. It was 10 times larger than Saturn's biggest ring and may extend 4–10 million miles around the planet. (Yep. Saturn *really* digs its jewelry.)

Happy to Meet All Three of You

When Galileo saw Saturn in his telescope in 1610, he thought he saw three celestial bodies waving back at him. (OK, they didn't wave. Saturn doesn't have arms, as far as we know.) He thought that Saturn was a system of one larger body and two smaller moon-like bodies. It was Christiaan Huygens, a Dutch astronomer, who peeped at Saturn in 1659 with a better telescope and concluded that Saturn is surrounded by rings.

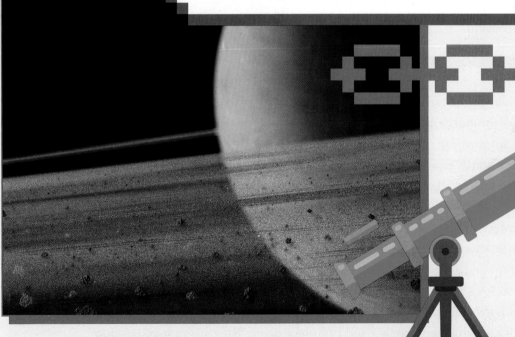

—Closeup of Saturn's rings

Saturn must scoff at us every time we do the wave in a football stadium, because it has a far bigger wave going on in its rings. As Saturn's moons orbit, they cause ripples in the rings, like throwing stones in a pond. But there are also ripples going in the opposite direction, which suggest that Saturn itself might be getting in on the wave action. Saturn might be oscillating (shaking back and forth), causing these ripples in its rings. Scientists are not quite sure what causes this oscillating, but when you look as good as Saturn, you've earned your right to dance your way through the solar system.

For Saturn's Next Magic Trick . . .

Once every 15 years, Saturn's rings pull a disappearing act on us. We can see Saturn's rings normally, because the rings reflect sunlight. But when Saturn moves into a certain spot in its orbit, the rings reflect very little sunlight and seem to disappear. This phenomenon is called *ring-plane crossing*.

December 1994

May 1995

—Saturn's ring-plane crossing

Besides the hexagon "hat" Saturn has on top of its north pole, there is also a mighty interesting phenomenon brewing in its south pole—a massive swirling polar vortex, resembling a gigantic hurricane. The dark eye of the storm is two-thirds the size of Earth. In 2008, the Cassini spacecraft took a magnificent photograph of this creepy and swirly dark eye.

If you love a good thunderstorm, you'll certainly get your fill on Saturn. Approximately once every Saturn year (29 Earth years), Saturn develops Great White Spots, which are Earth-sized thunderstorms. They are so massive that we can see them through telescopes. Scientists have observed these storms

Orbit It, Don't Spit It

Iapetus might be the saddest of Saturn's moons. This walnut-shaped moon is tidally locked, so it always presents the same face to Saturn, never turning away. It's also in a really unfortunate orbit. Although most of Iapetus is bright, its leading surface is mottled with dark splotches.

Scientists believe this dark material is ejected from nearby moons, including Phoebe. Imagine getting hit in the face with spitballs for millions of years, with no way to turn away!

—Iapetus

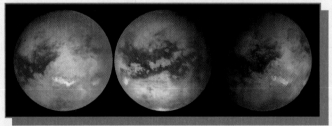

—Sides of Titan in infrared

Among Saturn's moons, Titan is clearly the big cheese. Larger than Mercury, Titan holds 96% of the material orbiting Saturn, including the rings. Titan is also the only known solar system body besides Earth with liquid on the surface. Titan's dense nitrogen atmosphere, 10 times taller than Earth's, rains methane and ethane, forming lakes and even seas on the surface.

Another of Saturn's moons looks ready for its Hollywood close-up. Mimas features a gigantic crater stretching over one third of its surface, giving it an uncanny resemblance to the *Star Wars* Death Star. (Don't worry. It's not a trap!) The impact that formed the crater likely almost ripped Mimas apart and fractured the moon's far side. Maybe the makeup department can help?

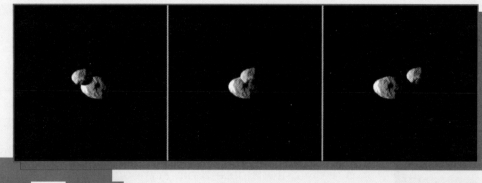

—Epimetheus dances in front of Janus

When it comes to wacky moon behavior, size isn't everything. Epimetheus and Janus are two potato-shaped moons, each around 100 miles wide, that orbit Saturn in a gap between rings. Circling less than 100,000 miles from the planet, the two moons complete a full orbit in 17 hours—but one is always a little faster than the other. That's because one moon orbits about 30 miles closer to Saturn than the other. Which moon is closer? That depends on when you look.

Every 4 years, the inner, faster-orbiting moon catches up to its outside neighbor, until the moons' mutual gravity wobbles their orbits. Like a square-dancing duo, they cartwheel past each other and change places—the inner moon on the outside, and the outer one inside. The swap takes 100 days, and then the new orbits stabilize—for about 4 years, when the dance begins again.

If Saturn's moons and rings seem like a "chicken or egg" question of which came first, the most likely answer is: yes. Some rings and moons appear to be young, while others are as old as Saturn. Some moons probably formed from dust and clods in the rings, and some rings likely grew from moons bumping into each other. But one interaction is clear—and very exciting.

Saturn's moon Enceladus sprays material into space, which forms the wide, hazy E ring. But it's what Enceladus is spewing, and from where, that makes scientists want a closer look. Enceladus is

—The fountain-like sources of the spray of material are visible when Enceladus is backlit by the sun

also looks like a pale blue dot. And from a-near, it looks like a pale blue planet. Uranus is greenish-blue all over, due to methane gas sprinkled in its atmosphere of hydrogen and helium.

—Earth resembling a "pale blue dot"

It's What's on the Inside That Counts

Although Uranus is closer to the sun than Neptune and receives more than twice as much solar energy, its surface temperature is actually slightly colder. That's because of differences in heat generated internally by the two planets. Neptune's core generates about 2.5 times as much energy as it receives from the sun, while Uranus generates only about as much as the sun provides. How that energy is generated, and why it differs so much, is currently unknown.

Like Saturn and Jupiter, Uranus is sometimes called a *gas giant* because of its dense atmosphere. But Uranus also qualifies as an *ice giant*—beneath the gas, most of the planet's mass comes from a thick mantle of water, methane, and ammonia ices. With all of that ice, it's no surprise Uranus's atmosphere is the coldest of all solar system planets, reaching lows at the cloud tops of nearly -360°F. Come to think of it, we'd probably turn blue, too.

Although far out in the solar system suburbs, Uranus isn't exactly lonely. The planet boasts 27 moons and 13 rings, two of which were found by the Hubble Space Telescope in 2005. The rings are thought to be remnants of a former moon broken apart by Uranus's gravity.

—This Voyager 2 image reveals a continuous distribution of small particles throughout the Uranus ring system

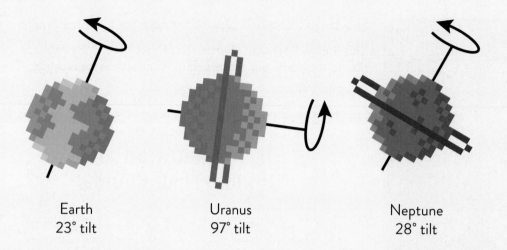

Earth
23° tilt

Uranus
97° tilt

Neptune
28° tilt

Uranus is also unique in that it's fallen and it can't get up. Uranus's spin axis doesn't point "up and down" with respect to its orbit, but in the same direction. In the early days of the solar system, two giant collisions with other bodies may have knocked Uranus onto its side. So although most planets twirl like graceful ballerinas as they orbit, Uranus topples end over end like a bowling ball. This orbital skew leads to very long days at Uranus's poles, each of which faces the sun for half of an 84-year orbit. That's 42 years of daylight, followed by 42 years of night!

You Call That a Wind?

Uranus's unique tilt also leads to extreme weather patterns. Voyager 2 happened to pass Uranus during its calm summer and saw little variation across the sur-face—but wild storms as large as North America with winds of 560 miles per hour have been observed via telescope. Still, Uranus's wacky weather has nothing on Neptune. Voyager observed an Earth-sized "Great Dark Spot" storm on Neptune with winds of 1,300 miles per hour—the strongest in the solar system!

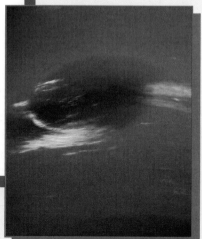

—Neptune's "Great Dark Spot"

Like Uranus, Neptune is an ice giant with a chilly atmosphere, a thick icy middle, and a rocky inner core. It shares Uranus's blue color—but for reasons unknown, Neptune's blue is much brighter. Because it orbits 2.8 billion miles away, give or take a light-minute, it takes 165 Earth years for Neptune to circle the sun. That means the one-Neptunian-year anniversary of its 1846 discovery was in 2011. Should we all meet up for a party when Neptune turns 2 in 2176?

Neptune's "moon posse" currently has 14 members, including a tiny new moon spotted in 2013. The largest moon, Triton, is the only major satellite in the solar system with a retrograde orbit, meaning it orbits Neptune in the opposite direction of the planet's rotation. Triton is also the coldest measured body in the solar system, around -390°F. On Voyager 2's 1989 flyby, it observed geysers on Triton shooting ice 5 miles into space!

—Triton

—Neptune's outermost ring matter mysteriously clumps into three arcs

Like a good outer planet, Neptune has a ring system—but as usual, the "out-there" planet does things differently. Neptune has five main rings, but the outer ring isn't a full circle. Instead, the ring's matter clumps into "arcs," with gaps between. The gravity of a nearby moon may be to blame—and observations show the outer rings may be breaking up and could one day disappear.

IS THAT A REAL THING?
Jupiter Is a Failed Star

Jupiter has a lot in common with our sun. They both consist of hydrogen and helium, and they are massive compared to the other planets in the solar system. But Jupiter is only 0.1% of the total mass of the sun. So, is Jupiter really a planet? Or is it star that never grew up?

Jupiter is definitely not a star, because it doesn't have enough mass to perform fusion, the process stars use to make energy. It also doesn't fit the description of a brown dwarf, an object that is a bit like a failed star. Scientists think brown dwarfs form like stars, but Jupiter formed in a very different way. Jupiter is also thought to have a solid core, and stars do not. So, Jupiter is considered the biggest planet in our solar system and not the second biggest star.

Jupiter and the sun do have something else in common besides their compositions, however. Due to their masses, they are both strong sources of gravity and have significant effects on the motion of planets, moons, and other solar system objects. Studying Jupiter's and the sun's formations could give scientists a better idea of how our entire solar system works.

Structure of Jupiter

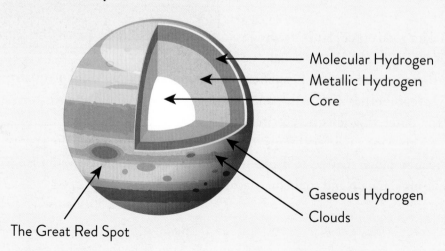

Molecular Hydrogen
Metallic Hydrogen
Core

Gaseous Hydrogen
Clouds

The Great Red Spot

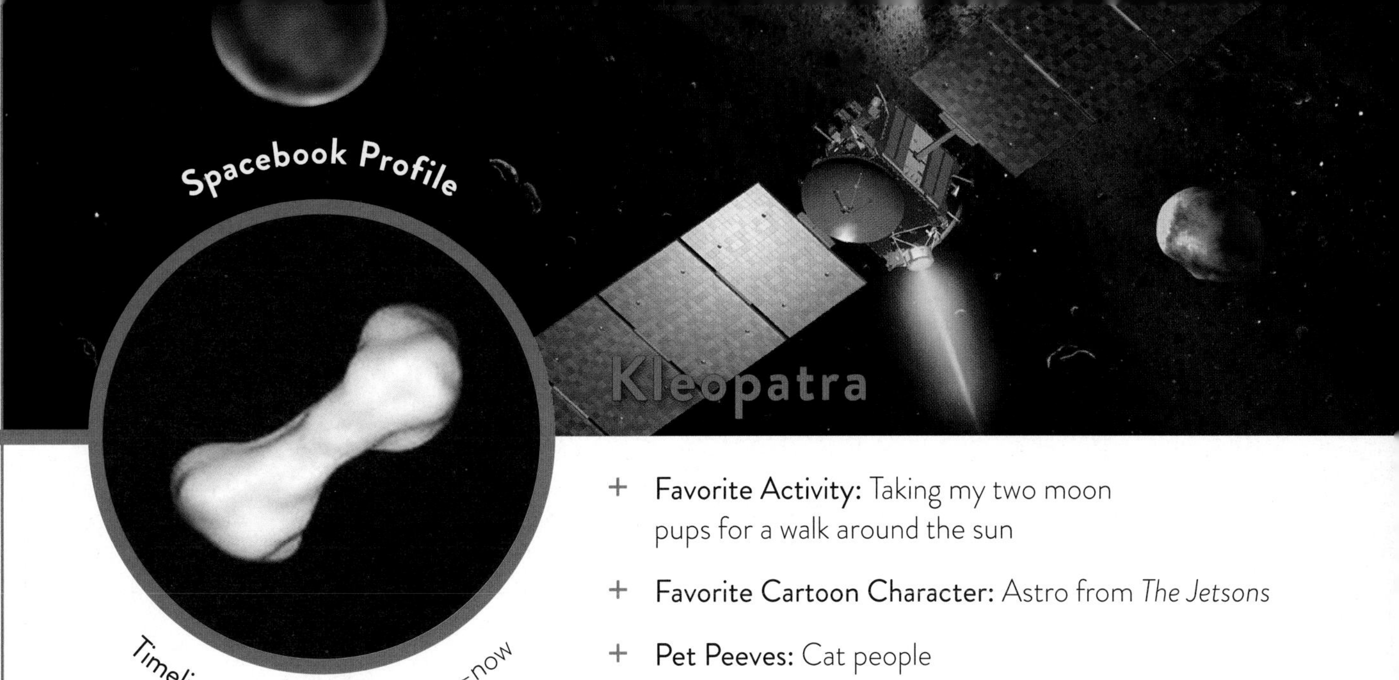

Kleopatra

+ **Favorite Activity:** Taking my two moon pups for a walk around the sun

+ **Favorite Cartoon Character:** Astro from *The Jetsons*

+ **Pet Peeves:** Cat people

Timeline: 4.6 billion years ago–now

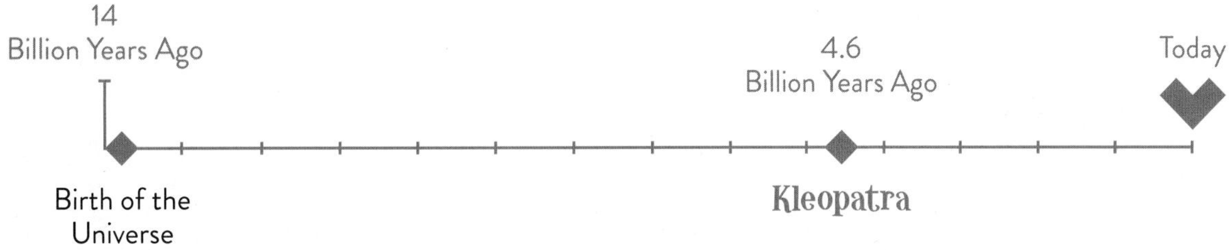

14
Billion Years Ago

4.6
Billion Years Ago

Today

Birth of the
Universe

Kleopatra

ASTEROIDS: THE REAL-LIFE VIDEO GAME

If you want to travel from Mars to Jupiter, things could get a little rocky. The asteroid belt formed with the rest of the solar system, and it's basically a collection of rocky remains. Scientists theorize that a planet started to form between Mars and Jupiter, but Jupiter's gravitational pull prevented one from forming. So now, the rest of us neat and orderly planets are stuck living with a big messy bedroom in the middle of our solar system. (Thanks, Jupiter.)

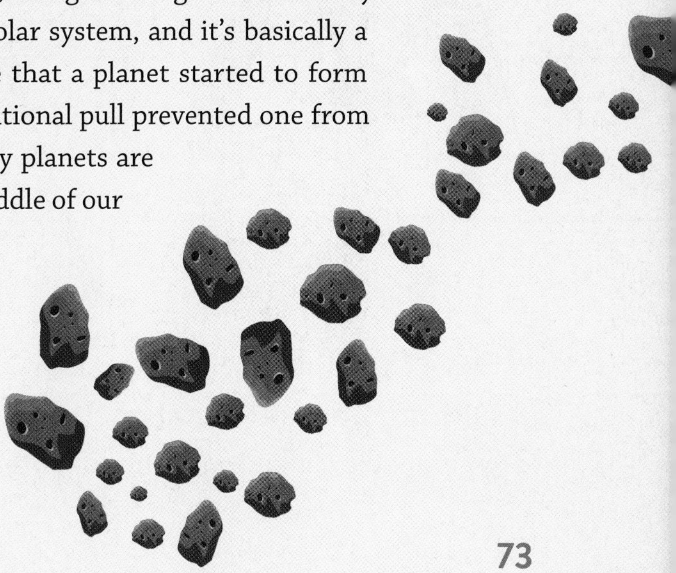

Asteroids tend to be oddly shaped, and many rotate in weird ways, clumsily tumbling as they orbit around the sun. Some asteroids even have small moons. The dog-bone-shaped asteroid Kleopatra has two satellite moons named Alexhelios and Cleoselene. Like stars, asteroids can even form binary relationships with each other, in which the two asteroids orbit around each other like two star-crossed lovers dancing.

Cooler Than Fairy Dust

In 2016, NASA launched OSIRIS-REx, which will retrieve dust samples from the near-Earth asteroid Bennu in 2018 and return to Earth in 2023. NASA invited people from around the world to have their names etched on a "Messages to Bennu!" microchip aboard OSIRIS-REx. More than 440,000 people have their names etched on the microchip.

—The OSIRIS-REx spacecraft is lifted at Cape Canaveral

—Osiris (left) is an ancient Egyptian god linked with transition, resurrection, and regeneration. The Bennu (right) is an ancient Egyptian deity linked with the sun, creation, and rebirth.

Most known asteroids are in the main asteroid belt between Mars and Jupiter. Outside of the belt, there are Trojan asteroids, which share an orbit with a planet but do not crash into it. Mars, Jupiter, and Neptune have Trojans, and NASA discovered Earth's first Trojan asteroid in 2011. (Wave hello!) Its name is 2010 TK7, and it was detected by NASA's NEOWISE project. There are also near-Earth asteroids, which cross Earth's orbit. Scientists keep a close watch on these, because some could be a threat if they entered Earth's atmosphere.

—Vesta

There is one habitant in the asteroid belt that really stands out from the crowd. Vesta is the second biggest object in the asteroid belt after the dwarf planet Ceres. Vesta is bright enough to even be seen with the naked eye on some nights. Its surface is much like our own moon's, and it has basaltic rock, which could only come from a volcanic eruption. It also has three layers—a crust, mantle,

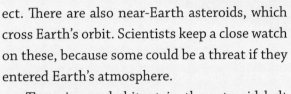

—Vesta's
wavy terrain

Singin' in the (Rocky) Rain

When asteroids or meteoroids (small pieces of asteroids) enter the Earth's atmosphere, they are called *meteors*. When they reach the Earth's surface, we call them *meteorites*. A group of scientists analyzed a bunch of meteorites found in Russia and concluded that most of them came from an asteroid collision that happened 466 million years ago. They even found meteorites from a collision that involved Vesta, the second largest object in the asteroid belt. That collision happened about 1 billion years ago.

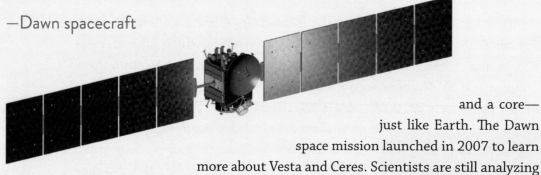

—Dawn spacecraft

and a core—just like Earth. The Dawn space mission launched in 2007 to learn more about Vesta and Ceres. Scientists are still analyzing the data from Vesta, but Vesta's unusual characteristics suggest it formed very early in our solar system's history. Vesta does have one fun feature—a series of circular craters connected to each other, largest to smallest. It's appropriately nicknamed the "Snowman."

Vesta isn't the only oddball in the asteroid belt. Another large asteroid, Themis, was the first asteroid discovered to contain water (more specifically, ice) on its surface. It also contains carbon-containing molecules. Water and carbon are vital to life on Earth, and scientists think pieces of Themis and similar asteroids may have brought more of these vital substances to Earth's surface.

20 km

—Vesta's "Snowman" craters

There Be Dragons! (And Dungeons, Apparently)

Early in 2017, NASA scientists spotted an asteroid that seems to have quite an affinity for tabletop gaming. The newly discovered asteroid 2017 BQ6 is quite angular, resembling the dice used to play the classic game Dungeons & Dragons. The scientists spotted bright spots on the asteroid, which may be boulders. Or the asteroid is just trying to show us its Charisma.*

*Please consult your nearest D&D manual for an explanation of that reference.

10 miles across. As the comet streaks toward the sun, it's warmed by the heat, which turns some of the solid ice—from water, carbon dioxide, methane, or other compounds—into gases. The gases form an atmospheric layer around the comet, called a *coma*.

This coma sticks close to the comet nucleus—at first. But as the comet barrels toward the sun, solar winds and radiation push the coma outward. Eventually, the comet forms two tails—one made of ionized gas, the other of loose dust—blown off of the back of the comet nucleus like a bad cowlick. Despite their small nuclei, cometary comas may be a million miles wide, with

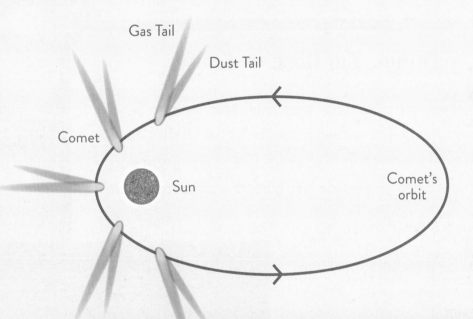

Gas Tail
Dust Tail
Comet
Sun
Comet's orbit

Tales of the Tails

If not for their tails, we might never detect comets—their nuclei are usually covered with black tar-like materials. Because the tails are pushed by solar radiation, they always point away—so tails "lead" comets flying away from the sun. When Earth passes through dust and rocks left by comet tails, we see meteor showers, as particles burn up in the atmosphere as "shooting stars."

tails 100 million miles long—all thanks to ice, and the "outgassed" material burned away from it.

Scientists have found around 5,000 comets—but those comets aren't all from the same place. Our solar system contains comets you might call "city cousins" and "country cousins." The city cousins begin life in a region called the *Kuiper belt*, around the orbit of Pluto. When gravity bumps a Kuiper belt comet into a closer orbit, it becomes a *short-period* comet. These comets take 200 years or fewer to make an orbit, and some can be tracked and predicted in detail.

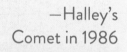

Things You Oort to Know

The Oort cloud has never been seen—it's so far away, and objects within it so small, that there's currently no way to confirm it's there. But the theory of a huge far-out cloud of billions of icy objects is the best explanation we have now for the origins of long-period comets. Some short-period comets, including Halley's, may have once been long-period Oort cloud comets.

—Halley's Comet in 1986

Way out in the solar suburbs are *long-period* comets. These country cousins live in a theorized area called the *Oort cloud*, a thousand times farther than the Kuiper belt and stretching 3 light-years from the sun! (A light-year is 5.9

When the IAU listed the new planethood requirements, it became clear right away that Pluto, listed as a planet for decades, didn't meet the criteria. Instead, Pluto was reclassified ("demoted," some said) to a dwarf planet. This upset some people, who were used to a nine-planet system.

An Astronomer's Dozen

As the IAU debated how to deal with the maybe-sort-of-but-not-quite-planetary discoveries piling up, they talked through a few different proposals. One of these suggested a solar system with 12 "official" planets—the eight we know today, plus Ceres, Pluto, Charon, and Eris (then called 2003 UB313). Under that system, which was rejected, and taking recent discoveries into account, we might have 14, 15, or as many as 20 solar system planets today!

—Charon

But nine planets weren't going to work any longer. Since Pluto's discovery in 1930, other findings chipped away at its special planetary status. First, Pluto turned out to be smaller than expected when its largest moon, Charon, was discovered to be a separate object and nearly half Pluto's size. The two rotate around each other, so if Pluto is a planet, then Charon should be, too.

So should Ceres, which was considered a planet for 50 years after its discovery in 1801. It was only "demoted" when other asteroids were discovered in its neighborhood. But the real nail in Pluto's planetary coffin was the discovery of Eris in 2003. Eris is roughly Pluto's size and further proof that in (and beyond) the Kuiper belt, many Pluto-like objects are waiting to be found.

How many should be "planets"? One? None? Forty-two? The dwarf planet category was a fair compromise.

Dwarf planets may be littler than "true" planets, but fascinating facts come in these small packages. Pluto, for example, has five moons and a large heart-shaped region on its surface, discovered by NASA's New Horizons probe in 2015. Half of this heart is a crater 600 miles wide, filled with frozen carbon monoxide and other ices. The crater may have formed from an asteroid impact 4 billion years ago. Pluto also spews methane gas toward its moon Charon, staining the moon's pole red.

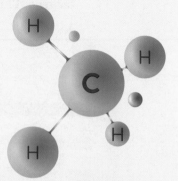

—Methane (top) and carbon monoxide (bottom)

New Dwarfs on the Block

Makemake and Haumea are ice-covered dwarf planets in the Kuiper belt, similar to Pluto but a bit smaller. Unlike Pluto, these objects were recently discovered (Haumea in 2004, Makemake in 2005), and no missions are currently planned to explore them up close. Makemake has one known moon, just 100 miles across, while football-shaped Haumea has two (Namaka and Hi'iaka), one of which may have broken off from Haumea after a violent ancient collision.

—How Haumea and its moons, Namaka (top left) and Hi'iaka (bottom right) are theorized to look

—Makemake with its moon, MK-2

explanation for why we see so many short-period comets from Earth. His theory was finally supported in 1992. After 5 years of peeping through the University of Hawaii's telescope, astronomers Dave Jewitt and Jane Luu caught sight of a teeny tiny red speck far past Pluto, about 44 AU from the sun. The first Kuiper belt object (or KBO) was discovered! The scientists nicknamed it Smiley, but its official name is 1992 QB1. (Yeah, we like Smiley better, too.)

—Gerard Kuiper

Finding a Needle in a Far, Far Away Haystack

In 2002, astronomers at the Palomar Observatory in San Diego made a big, icy discovery. They spotted a large Kuiper belt object, now known as *Quaoar* (pronounced "Kwa-war"), which is roughly half the size of Pluto. Quaoar was later found in photographs taken in 1980, but it wasn't noticed at the time. Quaoar has a long orbit around the sun—one trip takes about 288 years—and it's more than a billion miles past Pluto.

—Palomar Observatory

—How Quaoar and its moon Weywot are theorized to look

There are a few different types of objects found in the Kuiper belt and scattered disk region. The first are classical objects. Just like a classic movie feels comfortable and familiar, classical Kuiper belt objects don't have a lot of surprises. Their orbits follow paths similar to the planets, and scientists theorize that these objects' orbits haven't changed much over time.

We also have some choreographed dancers out there, called *resonant objects*. Resonant objects match up in ratios to another object's orbit, usually Neptune's. The most common is 2:3 resonance, meaning the object orbits the sun twice in the same amount of time it takes Neptune to orbit three times. Pluto and similar objects (called *plutinos*) are resonant objects. Pluto orbits exactly twice for every three Neptune orbits.

Look at the Pretty Colors

When scientists detect Kuiper belt objects, they tend to appear as tiny pixels of red, white, or blue light. Classical objects with nearly circular orbits (called *cold classicals*) are always red, and those with more pronounced elliptical orbits are white or blue. This is a bit of a head-scratcher, because many comets that originate from this region appear black due to the sun's radiation. Some scientists think that the classical Kuiper belt objects may exist in a zone where the charged particles from the sun are not strong enough to blacken these objects.

—Eris, the largest known scattered disk object, and its moon

Scattered disk objects, or SDOs, are a hot mess. Or, more accurately, a cold mess. They have highly eccentric orbits, and most of the time we can't see them because

solar wind (or *stellar wind*, for stars in general) that washes past the solar system.

This solar wind blows at an incredible rate—more than one million tons of material leave the sun every second, shooting in all directions at around one million miles per hour. It's the force of these charged plasma particles and their associated magnetic field that forms the sun's "bubble." Within the heliosphere, no stellar winds from other stars, (most) cosmic rays, or would-be galactic hitchhikers can sneak in. The constant gust of solar wind blows them away.

When Wind Gets Windier

All solar wind particles are speedy, but some are speedier than others. Scientists have identified slow solar winds—where "slow" means around 700,000 miles per hour, which would still totally get you a speeding ticket—and fast solar winds. The fast solar winds can travel nearly 1.8 million miles per hour and come from areas on the sun called *coronal holes*. These coronal holes appear dark on X-rays, and their high-speed winds can cause geomagnetic storms on Earth.

—An elongated coronal hole on the surface of the sun

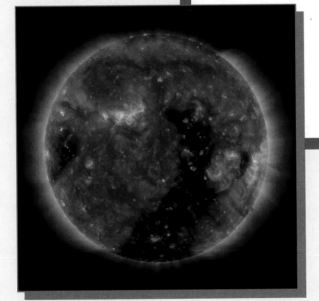

But the solar wind can't keep the speed up forever. Gradually, plasma particles slow, finally dropping below the speed of sound. This creates a shock wave—a cosmic sonic boom—out past the Kuiper belt, around 75–90 AU from the sun. This wave is called the *termination shock*, and it pushes particles outward, helping keep the heliosphere separate from outer space.

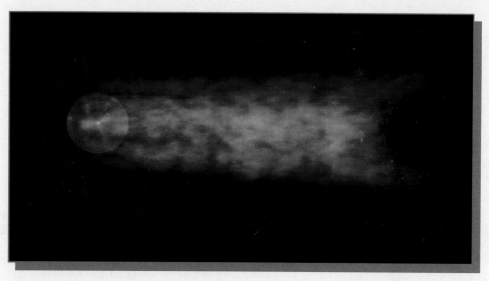

—The solar system's heliotail

The termination shock gives the solar system a buffer against the interstellar medium, but it's not the end of the heliosphere. Plasma from the sun keeps moving outward—but slower now, and intermingled with stellar and cosmic particles pushing in. This area is the heliosheath, and it becomes denser and hotter as pressure from outside stellar winds builds up. Finally, at the heliopause, around 120 AU from the sun, the solar wind gives out and the heliosphere ends.

Would You Believe "Near-Sphere"?

Although the heliosphere is less oblong than once believed, the termination shock does give it one predicted feature: a tail. Called the *heliotail*, it's not the stretchy comet-like tail astronomers imagined, but it does trail behind the heliosphere and is made of plasma jostled by the termination shock. Readings from NASA's IBEX satellite suggest that the heliotail is shaped like a four-leaf clover and changes over time, depending on the strength of the solar winds.

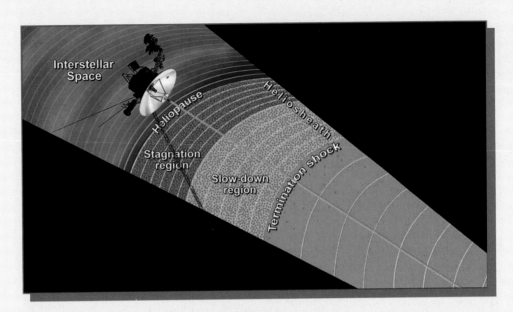

—This image depicts Voyager 1's path through the heliosphere and into interstellar space

No human has ever been outside the heliosphere, or even close to the edge—but one of our space probes has managed to escape, and others may soon follow. Launched on September 5, 1977, NASA's Voyager 1 flew by Jupiter and Saturn by 1980, and then was pointed toward interstellar space, rushing away from the sun at nearly 40,000 miles per hour.

(Hey, cut Voyager some slack. We can't all be solar wind particle speedsters.)

The fastest probe ever launched, Voyager 1 became the first spacecraft to cross the termination shock in 2004, and in 2012, Voyager 1's sensors detected an increase in charged particles from outside the solar system—indicating it had broken through the heliopause and into interstellar space! As of June 2017, Voyager 1 was more than 12 billion miles from the sun (over 138 AU, but who's counting?) and going strong.

Voyager 1's "twin," Voyager 2, also launched in 1977, is close behind. Voyager 2 entered the heliosheath in 2007, and may soon reach interstellar space. Both Voyagers are expected to function through at least 2020, but the same can't be said for 1970s probes Pioneer 10 and 11. Although far out (about 114 AU and 92 AU, respectively), contact with both was lost years ago.

IS THAT A REAL THING?
Planet X

For years, some people have worried about an unseen threat lurking in the void. They believe an undetected planet—often called Nibiru or Planet X—will swoop in from the outer solar system and wreak havoc, perhaps even colliding with Earth. This was first predicted (without scientific evidence) to occur in 2003. And when that didn't happen, in 2012. And again in 2016. Probably there's another disaster scheduled soon. We haven't checked.

Meanwhile, there's no actual evidence for a planet hurtling toward Earth. Astronomers would detect such an object years in advance. Also, any large body with an orbit swinging from beyond Neptune into Earth's path would be flung out into space. In short, there's no "Planet X."

That doesn't mean something isn't out there. In 2015, astronomers studying a group of Kuiper belt objects found that a planet-sized mass nearby would explain oddities in the objects' orbits. The theoretical planet, dubbed "Planet Nine," would be 10 times Earth's size and many times farther out than Neptune.

Today, astronomers scour the sky for Planet Nine. It wouldn't be the first planet found based on oddball orbital data—Neptune was spotted just where expected, based on quirks in Uranus's orbit.

This time, there's other evidence, too. The plane of the known planets' orbits is tilted slightly off the sun's axis—but no one knows why. One theory that fits the data: a planet orbiting at a 30-degree tilt, with a similar size and location as predicted above. Stay tuned, planet fans—the solar system may soon reveal another. (Happily, it won't be coming at Earth.)

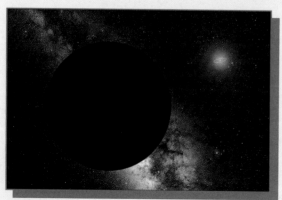

—How Planet Nine is theorized to look

—FROM PAGE 71...

Bizarre Space Trivia, Answer

The dwarf planet Ceres is one of several bodies in the solar system believed to have volcanoes that spew out:

a. Lava

b. Steam

c. Icy water (correct)

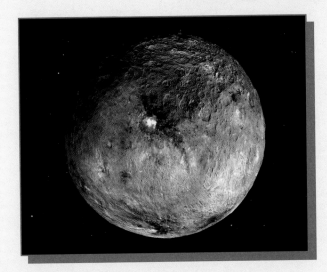

—This false-color image of Ceres shows the differences in surface materials

The Details: We think of volcanoes as boiling over with searing hot lava from deep underground—and on Earth, that's true. But on Ceres—and perhaps a few of the solar system's moons—the material under volcanoes isn't red-hot magma, or red-hot anything. Instead, it's a thick layer of ice. When tidal forces from gravity generate heat, some of that ice can deform, crack, and melt. In liquid (or ice cube) form, it shoots up toward the surface and erupts, just like lava in volcanoes on Earth. These ice volcanoes, or cryovolcanoes, pack the same punch, only at much cooler temperatures.

SECTION 4
Super-Duper Stars

Twinkle, twinkle, not-so-little stars. Stars may look like specks in our night sky, but make no mistake—they are large and in charge, especially in a gravitational sense. From Earth's BFF (the sun) to terrifying cannibal stars lurking in deep space, in this chapter you will learn why stars always make it to the top of the universe's A-list.

Bizarre Space Trivia

On a clear night, how many stars can you see with the naked eye?

- **a.** Thousands
- **b.** Hundreds of thousands
- **c.** Millions

— Find out the answer at the end of the section (p. 137)! —

Protostar

+ **Current Mood:** Feeling the pressure

+ **Location:** No idea, I can't see anything

+ **Favorite Song:** "Dust in the Wind"

Age: Just a few million years old–still a baby!

10 Million Years Ago	7.5 Million Years Ago	~3 Million Years Ago	Today
Rigel A	Betelgeuse	Protostar	

WHEN YOU SQUISH INTO A STAR

A star is basically a huge ball of bright, fiery plasma. But each star begins life as something entirely un-starlike: fog. Space fog, specifically—or something very close.

Most empty space between stars is just that: empty, with no air, no water, no runs, no hits, no errors, basically nothing at all. If you're looking for Waldo, he's probably not in space.

But some space neighborhoods aren't quite as empty. These are filled with gas—mostly hydrogen—and tiny particles of dust. Even in these regions, called *molecular clouds* (or *galactic dust bunnies*), the gas and dust

are mostly spread out. In some areas of a cloud, the space might just look a bit hazy, or still like an empty void.

But in other areas, gas and dust swirl into a dense fog. As particles get closer, the gravity between them grows stronger. Over a million years or so, the dust and gas form a clump, like snowflakes packed in a snowball. This core clump attracts more material—the more massive it gets, the stronger its gravitational pull. The core rotates as it grows, and a disc of extra material builds around the middle, like a tutu fringe on a twirling ballerina hippo. When the gravity pulling inward on the massive gassy core is too much, the core collapses—and from the fog, a star is born.

Congratulations, It's a Star!

Only about 1% of the hydrogen in our galaxy is found in molecular clouds. Still, these clouds can be huge—up to 600 light-years across and containing material millions of times more massive than the sun! Stars may form in many spots in these clouds, also known as *stellar nurseries*—but once they do, watch out! As a "baby" star develops, it releases energy and wind that drive away leftover gas and dust, breaking up the cloud nearby. Talk about a fussy newborn.

—One of the most prolific birthing grounds in our Milky Way galaxy, a nebula called RCW 49

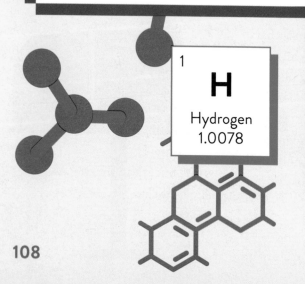

1
H
Hydrogen
1.0078

Strictly speaking, this blob of gravity-collapsed space stuff isn't yet a star. Rather, it's a protostar, where "proto" means "precursor" or "earliest form." It's becoming a star, but it's not there yet—the same way you could call a tadpole a "protofrog," or a bill (sitting there on Capitol Hill) a "protolaw." There's another step in the process, and for a protostar, it involves hydrogen.

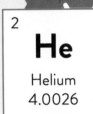

| 2 |
| **He** |
| Helium |
| 4.0026 |

—Two young brown dwarfs

Don't Let It Get You Brown

Not all cosmic gas balls emerge from stellar nurseries as stars. If a core isn't massive enough and its gravity is not so "squeezy," it won't grow dense enough to fuse much hydrogen into helium. This is a brown dwarf—a lukewarm gas glob that didn't quite find stardom. Brown dwarfs do shine a little, but they're much smaller, dimmer, and colder than true stars. That makes them hard to find, but scientists believe brown dwarfs may be as common as stars in our galaxy.

Think of a protostar as a big foam Nerf ball. Gravity pulls it inward, the way you might squeeze the ball in your hand. But you can only squeeze a Nerf ball so far. At some point, the foam can't squish any more.

Gravity, however, never lets up. And instead of Nerf foam, a protostar is made mostly of hydrogen, the smallest chemical element. Even so, at a certain squeezing point, hydrogen atoms truly can't get any closer without merging, like globs of pudding squishing together. So they do. The process is called *fusion*, but instead of Franken-pudding, two fused hydrogen atoms make a helium atom—and an awful lot of energy. Fusion also makes a protostar a star . . . almost.

Squishing atoms together is a neat trick for a protostar—but it's so much more. Once the fusion reaction takes off, everything changes, including what the protostar is made of. It's like learning a card trick that also turns you into chocolate—only much hotter, and far less delicious.

The fusion of two hydrogen atoms into a helium atom releases energy, including heat. Each event makes the protostar core a tiny bit hotter—but there are an octodecillion hydrogen atoms in an average star. That's a 10 followed by 57 zeros, and every pair in there can fuse to raise the temperature a tad. If you've ever been scolded for nudging the thermostat up a degree, what would happen if you did it half an octodecillion times?

—The star in the center, known as V1331 Cyg, is a young star that is starting to contract

Rock the Plasma! Rock the Plasma!

Three of the four fundamental states of matter are probably familiar: solid, liquid, and gas. The fourth state, plasma, seems rarer—but only on Earth. Plasma is formed from atoms of gas that are ionized, or stripped of electrons, creating an electric charge. You may see plasma in lightning, neon signs, TVs, and a few other places. But beyond Earth, the plasma in stars, and in the spaces between stars and galaxies, may make up 99% of all ordinary matter in the universe.

—Octodecillion

10,000,000,000,000,000,000,000,000,000,
000,000,000,000,000,000,000,000,000,000

When astronomers first analyzed the spectra of stars, they catalogued the different-looking patterns using an alphabetic code. The "plainest" spectra with few bands were assigned "A," with more complex patterns getting other letters up through "Q." For classifying patterns of spectral bands, the system worked great. But it didn't say anything about the stars themselves.

Superstars in Their Field

—Annie Jump Cannon

Annie Jump Cannon and around 80 other women worked in the late 1800s and early 1900s as star-cataloguing assistants to astronomer Edward Pickering at the Harvard College Observatory. At a time when few women were given the opportunity to contribute in the workplace, these "Harvard computers" crunched data, pored over sky charts, catalogued hundreds of thousands of stars, and developed stellar classification systems still in use today.

In 1911, astronomer Annie Jump Cannon began rearranging the existing groups based on specific spectral bands. The new set of jumbled letters was a tongue-twister—OBAFGKM—but it matched up with the temperatures and colors of the stars it described, with O stars the hottest and bluest and M stars red and relatively cool.

Within each class, stars are numbered from 0–9, based on decreasing temperature. So an F0 star is hotter than an F1, but an A9 star is hotter than both. Modern systems also add Roman numerals for luminosity, or the energy given off by a star, from I (supergiants) to V (dwarf stars).

These factors allow scientists to describe most stars we know of. Rigel A is a B8I star, so it's a very hot (though not among the hottest B-class stars), very luminous supergiant. The sun is a yellow G2V dwarf, while the next-closest star, Proxima Centauri, is a teeny M6V red dwarf.

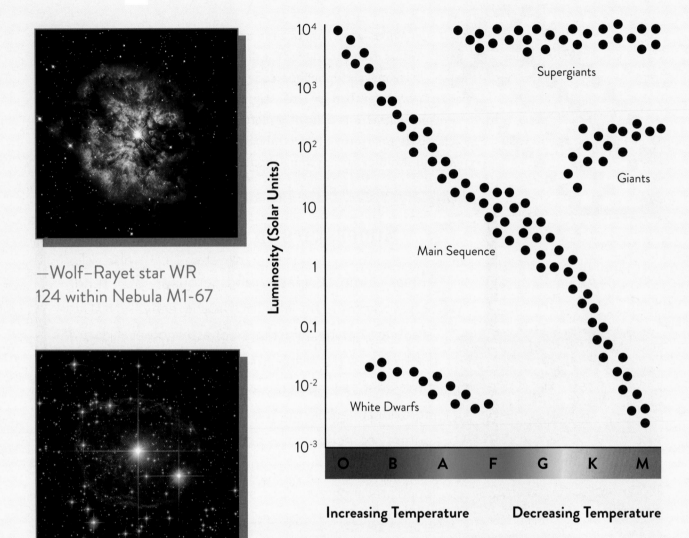

—Wolf–Rayet star WR 124 within Nebula M1-67

—Wolf–Rayet star WR 31a within an uncataloged Wolf–Rayet nebula

The OBAFGKM system—which Cannon suggested to memorize with the mnemonic "Oh Be a Fine Girl/Guy, Kiss Me," but which we prefer to remember as "Oh Boy, Another Far-out Galactic Kooky Mnemonic"—covers most stars in the sky. From the coolest, 2,400-degree red dwarf, to orange stars, to yellow stars, to white stars, to the blue blazing supergiant of 40,000-plus degrees, all have a place inside OBAFGKM. (Gesundheit.) But a few stars don't.

Astronomers have found some oddballs out there in space that don't follow the neat and simple rules we hoped they would. Wolf-Rayet stars, for instance, have no hydrogen bands in their spectra. Considering stars are made of and fueled by hydrogen, this is strange and unusual. Wolf-Rayet, or W-class, stars may be doomed supergiants that have used up their internal

Red giant stars are puffed up wide and made of layers of material, like giant jawbreakers. Some of the layers produce energy from fusion—but not always the same amount, or at the same rate. Because of this, many red giant stars are "variable"—they grow and shrink in size and brightness, pulsing as energy ebbs and flows within them. Talk about "dancing with the stars"!

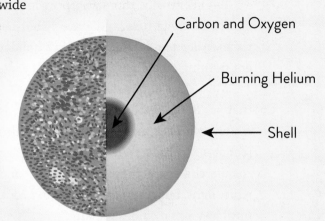

Carbon and Oxygen

Burning Helium

Shell

Too Dead to Go Red?

Not all stars go through a red giant phase—or so scientists believe. According to calculations, very small stars—roughly one-third the sun's mass or smaller—shouldn't have enough "extra" hydrogen to generate a new round of fusion, and gravity shouldn't compress them enough to fuse larger elements. But a star that small will take nearly one trillion more years to burn through its hydrogen, before we can observe what really happens. Waiting is so hard!

Stars can spend a billion years or more in the red giant phase, but they're not particularly stable. As layers of fusible elements run out, bits of the star get blown away and lost, others get crunched by gravity, and—if the star is dense enough—heavier elements are fused as star fuel.

But eventually, there's nothing left to burn. The elements left in the star are too heavy to fuse, and gravity squishes them into a dense clump. And we mean *really* dense. Your grandma's holiday fruitcake may seem dense, but it's got nothing on dying stars known as *white dwarfs*.

Most stars under eight solar masses—that is, 8 times our sun's mass—die as white dwarfs, crammed by gravity into planet-sized balls. White dwarfs are like cosmic charcoal—they give off heat and white light, but gradually darken and cool, until just a cold cinder remains.

—PK 329-02.2, a white dwarf, sheds its last outer layers into space, which appear as glowing clouds of gas called planetary nebulae

Eventually, Bet on Black

White dwarf stars are basically bare, spent cores of former stars, radiating light and heat but not producing any new energy from atomic fusion. Surface gravity may be around 100,000 times what we experience on Earth. The end for these once-stars is thought to be the *black dwarf* stage; black dwarfs are just white dwarfs that no longer give off any heat or light. In other words, cosmic gravel. But the first white dwarfs won't reach this stage for billions of years.

Becoming a white dwarf may not sound great, but trust us—low-mass stars have it easy. In stars with more than about eight solar masses, elements fuse and re-fuse until their cores fill with iron, which stars can't fuse—so they collapse, violently. Ever hear of "the harder they fall"?

In massive stars, gravity squeezes the core so tight that subatomic particles bleed together. This forms a *neutron star*, a

Best Light Show on Earth

The sun ejects bursts of charged particles. Most of these particles that head toward Earth are deflected by Earth's strong magnetic field, but when a large burst of particles occurs, the particles can trickle into the atmosphere at the poles. The particles excite the oxygen and nitrogen in our atmosphere, which eventually release this energy as photons (light particles), creating the pretty red, blue, and green colors in the sky during the northern and southern lights.

—Solar activity along the right side of the sun

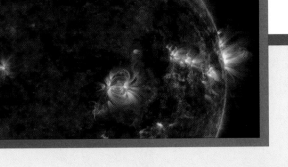

—The northern lights in Fairbanks, AK

The sun makes up about 99.8% of the entire mass in the solar system, and all of the planets, moons, comets, asteroids, and whatever-elses make up the other 0.2%. As the undisputed king of our solar system, the sun has a lot of influence over us. New research by NASA published in May 2016 found that the activity of a young sun may have helped to heat up the Earth, warming the planet enough to support life.

Back then, the sun was not as bright as it is today, and the Earth was only receiving about 70% of the energy from the sun that it does now. But the sun was much more active with superflares erupting regularly on the sun's surface. A solar flare is an eruption of energy on the sun's surface. Superflares are even larger, and they release a *lot* of energy. Today, we only experience a solar superflare once every 100 years or so, but the adolescent sun created up to about 10 superflares a day.

Keeper of the Peace

In 1967, the United States and the Soviet Union were in the middle of the Cold War. On May 23 of that year, several of the United States' missile radars became jammed. Willful disruption of these radars was considered an act of war, and the U.S. thought the Soviets were behind it. They immediately prepared to release aircraft with nuclear weapons into the sky, but space weather forecasters managed to inform the officials in the nick of time that the jam was caused by a solar flare.

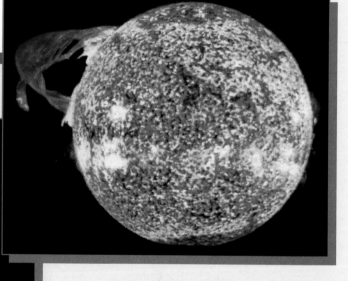

—In December 1973, Skylab 4 observes one of the most spectacular solar flares ever recorded

—One of NASA's most recent images of a solar flare

red supergiant. If this happened, Betelgeuse would have caught some of the momentum from the star's orbit, causing Betelgeuse to rotate faster.

Scientists don't know when Betelgeuse will go supernova, but the evidence indicates it will be sooner rather than later ("sooner" meaning anytime between tonight and thousands of years from now). To the naked eye, Betelgeuse will get a lot brighter in the sky. Scientists will see a lot more in their telescopes, and they are anxiously waiting for the show. (We presume they've already tried saying its name three times.)

—Betelgeuse; this is the first image of the surface of a star in the highest resolution available

How Do We Know What We Know?

Humans have been studying stars for centuries. The development of bigger and more powerful telescopes has given a much closer look at these stars and may help us understand the formation of our universe. Amateur astronomers can also help find new stars and even planets. In 2012, NASA reported that a pair of amateur astronomers from the Planet Hunters project found a Neptune-sized planet in a quadruple star system called Kepler-64b. The planet was named PH1B for Planet Hunters 1.

IS THAT A REAL THING?
Killer Solar Flares

In 2012, many people were mighty scared of the sun. The fear was caused by the ending of the Mayan calendar, which some believed forecasted the end of the world. During this time, the sun was also experiencing heightened activity due to its solar cycle. Some people feared that the sun could burn the Earth with a killer solar flare.

Solar flares do pose a threat, but not in the "gigantic hot ball of instant death" sort of way. Solar flares are powerful eruptions on the sun. Earth's magnetic field protects us from a lot of the sun's radiation, but a large solar event could disrupt satellites and communication equipment, causing widespread power outages. With everyone out there tweetbooking, face-paging, and insta-tumbling their lives, a major solar event could severely threaten our ever-connected way of life.

Scientists do know that the sun goes through cycles of high and low activity, so they watch the sun closely for changes. Many scientists are working with politicians to implement safeguards in our power grids and satellites to protect against damage. The U.S. Air Force has dedicated solar analysts monitoring the sun's activity every day, looking for activity that may interfere with airplanes and other military equipment. Monitoring the sun will help us predict solar events better and even come up with better ways to safeguard against them.

—FROM PAGE 105...

Bizarre Space Trivia, Answer

On a clear night, how many stars can you see with the naked eye?

a. **Thousands** (correct)

b. Hundreds of thousands

c. Millions

The Details: There are bajillions of stars in the universe. (Unfortunately, bajillion is not an official scientific measurement. But there are still a lot of stars out there!) Despite country singers and emo rockers crooning about sitting under millions of stars, we can only see a few thousand stars with our naked eyes. And the actual count varies widely. City dwellers see fewer due to city lights, and a bright full moon cuts down on the number of stars you see.

In 2006, NASA and the Canadian Space Agency worked with students like you on a project called Star Count. Students from all over North America counted the number of stars in the sky and entered their counts, their locations, and information about visibility conditions into a database. The information was used by scientists to assess light pollution.

SECTION 5
Life's Better in the Milky Way

The Milky Way is our galaxy. There are many galaxies like it (and many that aren't), but this one is ours. And as huge as our solar system is, it's barely a pinprick on the Milky Way map. In this chapter, we expand our horizons, several million times over, to tour the galaxy for the strangest, shockingest, and head-scratchingest mysteries of the Milky Way.

—Voyager 1

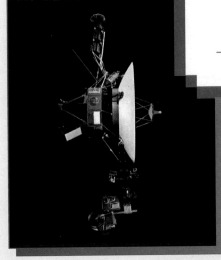

Bizarre Space Trivia

Voyager 1, launched in 1977, has escaped the solar system, traveling around 38,000 miles per hour. At that rate, how long would it take Voyager 1 to reach the Milky Way's center?

a. 450 years

b. 450,000 years

c. 450,000,000 years

— Find out the answer at the end of the section (p. 171)! —

The Milky Way

+ **Favorite Activity:** Spinning 'round like a record

+ **Favorite Food:** Other galaxies

+ **Frenemy:** Andromeda (Seriously, dude. Get away from me.)

Timeline: 13.2 billion years ago–now

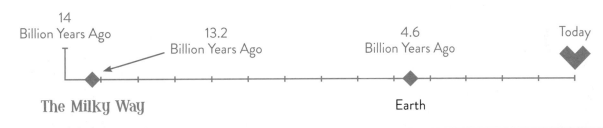

| 14 Billion Years Ago | 13.2 Billion Years Ago | 4.6 Billion Years Ago | Today |

The Milky Way   Earth

THE DIARY OF A NOT-SO-WIMPY GALAXY

It's nearly impossible to look at a picture of the Milky Way galaxy and not feel incredibly small, especially when our entire solar system barely looks like a dust speck in the middle of this big, beautiful Tilt-a-Whirl. But how did this galactic carnival ride form, anyway?

Scientists theorize that after the universe formed, there were pockets of gas around that eventually formed into clumps. This clumping allowed some of these pockets to heat up and eventually become stars. A *globular cluster* is a massive system of ancient stars. They are some of the oldest star systems in our galaxy, and they tend to group

141

together in spheres. Each spherical cluster could contain up to a million stars. There are more than 150 globular clusters in the Milky Way, and about a third are found concentrated near the center of the galaxy. In our galaxy, these clusters form a sphere pattern, which suggests that the early Milky Way may have been shaped like a ball before it grew and became the giant pinwheel it is today.

—Globular cluster

The name Milky Way originally referred to the white cloud-like patch that appears in our night sky. Ancient people were not sure what this patch was. Aristotle believed that it was the atmosphere on fire. (Fortunately, he was wrong.) In the 1600s, Galileo confirmed through his telescope that this patch was made up of stars. Today, we know this patch is a glimpse of the Milky Way, and it tells us a lot about our place in the galaxy. In fact, the word *galaxy* stems from the Greek word *galactos*, which means "milk."

Crying Over Spilled Milk

Ancient people had many theories about the white patch in the sky they called the Milky Way. One of the most famous depictions is *The Origin of the Milky Way*, a painting made by Italian artist Jacopo Tintoretto sometime between 1575 and 1580. Per Greek mythology, Hera (the goddess of fertility) tried to nurse baby Heracles. However, he was too strong, and Hera spilled her milk, creating the Milky Way.

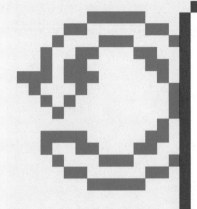

Hitch a Ride on the Crazy Carousel

Scientists estimate that the Milky Way galaxy spans 80,000 to 120,000 light-years, and our sun is located about 26,000 light-years from the center. Our solar system orbits the galaxy at 515,000 miles (or 829,000 kilometers) per hour. Even at this super-fast speed, it takes 230 million years for our solar system to make one trip around the Milky Way.

—The Milky Way

The Milky Way patch in our sky looks like a thin strip, which suggests our galaxy has a disk shape. It also goes around our entire planet, so we're not on the very edge of the galaxy. Because we have a whole bunch of galaxy around us, we're probably somewhere in the middle of the galaxy (between the center and the edge). If we were near the center of the galaxy, this strip would look a lot bigger in our sky, and we might even be able to see the center of the galaxy.

American astronomer Harlow Shapley (1885–1972) gave further evidence to our location when he noticed that the globular clusters in our sky seemed to form a sphere pattern, and they were all located in one specific point of the night sky—right around the constellation Sagittarius. He thought these spheres likely pointed to the center of the galaxy, and we now know his theory was correct.

Like all large galaxies, the Milky Way is a cannibal, meaning it grew to its size by devouring other galaxies. Traces of these old, eaten galaxies remain in the Milky Way, kind of like bug parts in a spider's web. And the Milky Way may be in the middle of another meal. Scientists think that the nearby Canis Major galaxy will eventually be ripped apart by the strong gravitational force from the Milky Way.

—Earth's location within the Milky Way

The Fault in Our Poop-Finding Stars

Dung beetles love their poop. They roll it up in balls and push it over great distances to their personal poop pantries. After a few tests in their natural habitat, researchers put the beetles in a planetarium and observed their poop-rolling paths under different star conditions. The beetles' paths were the straightest when all the stars were turned on, and almost as straight when only the Milky Way patch was turned on. This suggests that these beetles may rely on the Milky Way to navigate their late-night poop rolling.

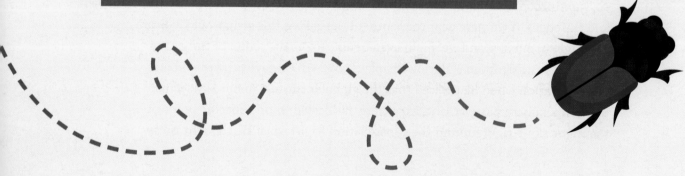

Getting Dizzy Playing Halo

The Milky Way is surrounded by a halo made up of old stars, globular clusters (ancient star systems), dark matter, and a lot of hot gas. This halo was once thought to be stationary, but in 2015, researchers found that the hot gas in the halo was spinning at the same rate of speed as the galaxy's disk. This finding can help astronomers understand more about how galaxies form and predict future changes to our galaxy.

From its center, our galaxy spreads out in a long, flat disk. Our disk is approximately 100,000 light-years long and 10,000 light-years thick. (Yep, you're living in a gigantic pancake.) Scientists estimate that there are 200 billion stars in the galaxy, and a few stars are added to our galaxy each year. The most common are red dwarf stars, which are dinky stars that are only one-tenth the size of our sun.

Our Milky Way galaxy also has an estimated 100 billion planets. Planets that orbit a star other than the sun are called *exoplanets,* and they are recent discoveries in the science world. On January 9, 1992, astronomers Alex Wolszczan and Dale Frail announced the first two confirmed exoplanets orbiting a star other than our own. The star was a pulsar located in the constellation Virgo, 2,300 light-years from Earth.

—How the sizes of exoplanets compare to Mars and Earth

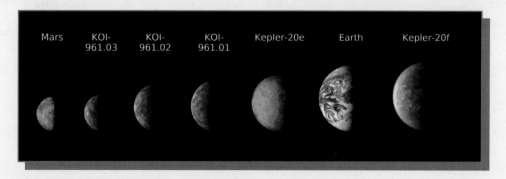

Maybe We Should Stop and Ask for Directions?

Hydrogen is the most abundant element in space. Recently, a group of scientists used hydrogen and two of the world's largest telescopes (the CSIRO radio telescope in Australia and the Max Planck telescope in Germany) to create the most detailed map of our galaxy to date. The project took 10 years and millions of observations to complete.

1
H
Hydrogen
1.0078

—The CSIRO radio telescope

—The Max Planck telescope

The Milky Way has long spiral arms, which have puzzled scientists for decades. The Milky Way spins very fast, so it would make sense that the arms would wind up around the center. But the arms of the galaxy do not. Also, each arm can't be made of the same stars for the entire orbit. If they were, it would mean the stars on the very edge of the galaxy moved a lot faster to keep

stars, blown away as the stars evolved or died in nova or supernova blasts. The "exploded" nebulae tend to be clearer in shape, although they grow fuzzier over time.

One famous nebula is the Orion Nebula, a star-forming cloud 1,300 light-years away. It's one of the few nebulae easily visible with the naked eye, located in the Orion constellation, below Orion's belt. (As a fluffy pinkish cloud there, you might call it "Orion's tutu.") Besides its beauty, the nebula is a happening place. One thousand stars may be forming there, and recent studies suggest the nebula also contains many planet-sized objects and possibly a black hole.

Just because (most known) nebulae are bright doesn't mean they're warm.

—Orion Nebula

—Eagle Nebula; the Pillars of Creation are visible in the nebula's bright white center

Pity the Pillars

Another star-forming nebular region is (probably) no more. In the Eagle Nebula 7,000 light-years away, a region called the *Pillars of Creation* was made famous by photos snapped by the Hubble Space Telescope. These majestic towers are several light-years tall and a sight to behold—but are likely already gone. A 6,000-year-old supernova nearby has likely wiped the pillars away—but the light from their destruction won't reach Earth for another thousand years.

Scientists have dubbed one nebula the coldest place in the universe. That's the Boomerang Nebula, an example of *planetary nebulae* that form when small stars blow off their outer layers in nova explosions.

In the Boomerang Nebula, around 5,000 light-years away, the cloud is acting like coolant in a refrigerator as it expands. That makes the nebula even colder than empty space, a chilly -458°F. We'd send the Boomerang Nebula a sweater, but we don't know its size.

Still, there are worse things than cold. The planetary Calabash Nebula is 5,000

—Boomerang Nebula

Nebula With a Nightlight?

Most of the nebulae we can observe are in the Milky Way—but there are exceptions. One type of extragalactic nebula, called an *enormous Lyman-alpha nebula*, or ELAN, can be 2 million light-years across and is usually found by the light of nearby quasars (see p. 184) or other high-energy sources. But in early 2017, the brightest-yet ELAN, found 10 billion light-years away, had no obvious source of light. So far, its bright but far-away shining remains a mystery.

light-years from Earth, but its issue isn't heat—it's smell. The gases in the Calabash Nebula have high sulfur content, making it stink to, well, high space. It's even been dubbed the "Rotten Egg Nebula." Ew.

Planetary nebulae are created from nova explosions of medium-sized stars—but a super-sized star dies in a truly super explosion, a *supernova*, which forms a nebula by shooting material outward at more than

—Calabash Nebula

16
S
Sulfur
32.066

60 million miles per hour. Supernova remnant nebulae dissipate into space over the course of a few million years and are some of the universe's few sources of heavy elements.

Because supernovae are so explosive, astronomers can watch remnant nebulae grow and change—sometimes right from the explosion! In February 1987, a star 166,000 light-years away exploded in a supernova, which could be seen by the naked eye for months afterward. Since then, astronomers have traced the nebula, shock waves, and rings of material shot into space.

Even when (modern) astronomers miss the "main event," supernova nebulae can provide fascinating views. Thirty years of data on Tycho's remnant, from a supernova observed in 1572, show a spongy mass of gas roiling through space. Likewise, the SN 1006 remnant (1006 A.D.), Crab Nebula (1054 A.D.), Kepler remnant (1604 A.D.), and more have been linked to supernovae recorded throughout history. For "cosmic glitter," nebulae are worth their weight in gold.

—The Crab Nebula is one of the most intricately structured and highly dynamic objects ever observed. This new image was assembled from 24 individual exposures taken with the Hubble Space Telescope.

—The first depiction of the Crab Nebula, in 1844

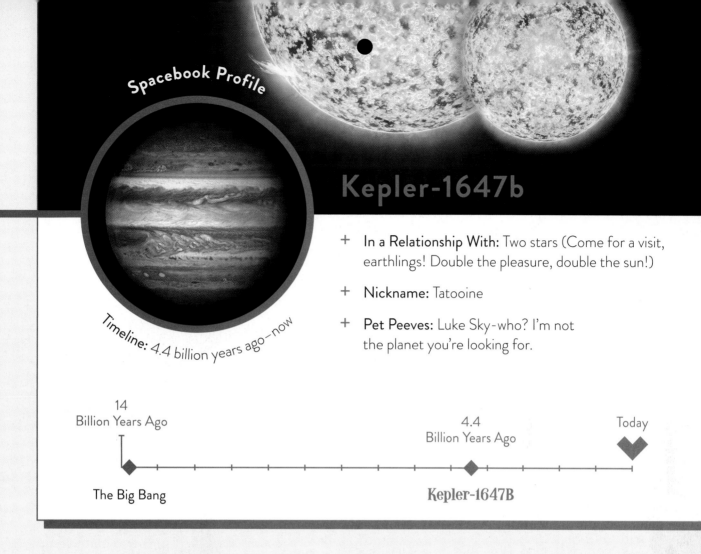

Kepler-1647b

- **In a Relationship With:** Two stars (Come for a visit, earthlings! Double the pleasure, double the sun!)

- **Nickname:** Tatooine

- **Pet Peeves:** Luke Sky-who? I'm not the planet you're looking for.

Timeline: 4.4 billion years ago–now

14 Billion Years Ago	4.4 Billion Years Ago	Today
The Big Bang	Kepler-1647B	

OUR CRAZY EXO-GIRLFRIENDS AND BOYFRIENDS

—This artist's concept depicts the pulsar planet system discovered by Alex Wolszczan in 1992

For decades, scientists wondered what magnificent worlds exist outside our very, very, *very* tiny corner of the galaxy. In 1992, we got an answer. Scientists discovered our first exoplanet, so named because it orbits a star other than the sun. Today, there are more than 1,000 confirmed exoplanets, and scientists keep finding more.

Why does finding a new exoplanet make scientists squeal and somersault over their telescopes? (Aside from the fact that some scientists are just squealy and somersaulty in

159

general. We don't let those scientists near the *really* expensive telescopes.) For one, an exoplanet is quite hard to find, especially compared to a star. A star gives off its own light, so we can see stars that are trillions of miles away. Planets do not, and they are also a fraction of the mass of the gigantic stars they orbit. Scientists need to look quite hard to find an exoplanet, so when one is finally found and confirmed, a great big cosmic conga line erupts in the space lab (probably started by the squealy and somersaulty scientist who almost broke the telescope).

The discovery of a new exoplanet can also get us closer to answering an age-old question: Are we alone out here? Scientists are especially interested in planets that exist in habitable zones, meaning they are the right distance from their stars to support liquid water on their surfaces, a necessary feature for life as we know it.

Dude, I Need My Space

In 2014, NASA found an exoplanet with a remarkable orbit around the star GU Piscium (so named because it is in the Pisces constellation). Called *GU Piscium b*, the planet orbits 2,000 AU from its star. (Remember: Earth orbits 1 AU from the sun, so that's pretty dang far!) To put it in perspective, Neptune takes 164.79 years to orbit the sun. GU Piscium b takes about 163,000 years to orbit its star!

—An Astronomical Unit, (AU)

1 AU = The distance from Earth to the sun

—The planet GU Piscium b and its star GU Piscium composed of visible and infrared images

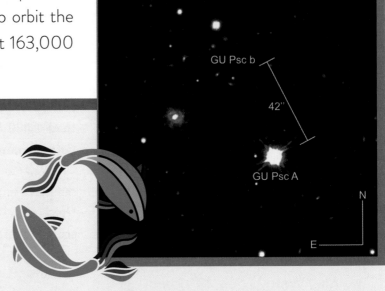

GU Psc b

42"

GU Psc A

N

E

The Magnificent Exo-Seven

—Spitzer Space Telescope

In early 2017, NASA's Spitzer Space Telescope made a record discovery in the constellation Aquarius. It detected seven Earth-sized exoplanets orbiting around a single star. The system is called *TRAPPIST-1*, named for the Transiting Planets and Planetesimals Small Telescope in Chile, which detected two of the confirmed seven planets in May 2016. This discovery is the first group of planets of this size located in the habitable zone.

—This artist's concept shows what the TRAPPIST-1 planetary system may look like, based on available data about the planets' diameters, masses, and distances from the host star

Scientists are quite interested in the atmospheres of exoplanets because they can give signs of possible life on the planet's surface. Living things alter the atmosphere on Earth. For example, plants release oxygen into the atmosphere through photosynthesis (the process in which plants make usable energy from the sun). Also, some gases, like methane, can be emitted by organisms as a part of basic life processes. Astronomers look at exoplanet atmospheres for specific substances, which might indicate that life exists there. In July 2016, the Hubble telescope studied the atmospheres of the first two exoplanets discovered in the TRAPPIST-1 system. Scientists found that they most likely do not have the hydrogen-heavy atmospheres that are found around gas giants. Because these planets exist in a habitable zone of their star, this increases the likelihood these planets could support life.

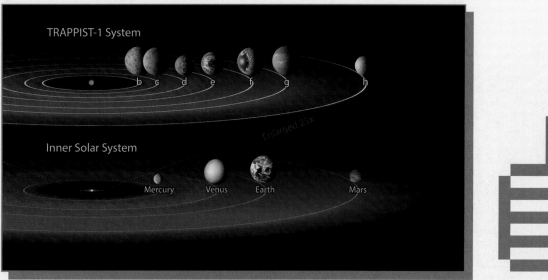

—Three exoplanets in the TRAPPIST-1 system, TRAPPIST-1e, f, and g, dwell in their star's habitable zone, which is a band around every star (shown in green) where temperatures are just right for liquid water to pool on the surface of an Earth-like world

But how do scientists even find an exoplanet to study at all? Do they just swing their telescopes around wildly, hoping to get lucky? (They do not. Mostly because these telescopes are really, *really* big.) Exoplanets do give clues that scientists can detect. The first sign is a wobbly star. Gravity works two ways in planet-star systems—the star pulls on the planet, and the planet pulls on the star. Looking for wobbly stars could give scientists a clue that there is a planet nearby tugging on them. Sometimes, it's possible to even catch an exoplanet in transit, as it passes in front of its star. The first exoplanet that was caught in transit occurred in 1999. The planet, nicknamed Osiris, has racked up quite a few first discoveries. It was also the first found to have an atmosphere that has carbon and oxygen, and it was one of the first exoplanets to be analyzed with spectroscopy, a technique that analyzes light and other types of waves to determine what makes up a space object.

Composition of the sun by mass

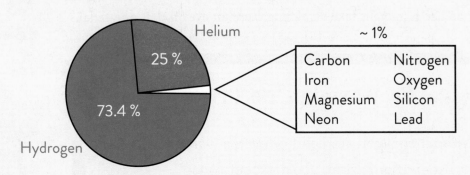

Helium

25 %

~ 1%

Carbon	Nitrogen
Iron	Oxygen
Magnesium	Silicon
Neon	Lead

73.4 %

Hydrogen

—Clumps of cold gas
across the Milky Way

Who Gassed Up the Galaxy?

Even the (not so empty) space in our galaxy is mysterious. In 2016, scientists found that radio waves from a distant quasar (see p. 184) were affected by never-before-seen clumps of cold gas in the Milky Way. These clumps of sneaky gas are hard to spot, but they could be scattered throughout the galaxy and make up a large part of its mass. Was it something the Milky Way ate?

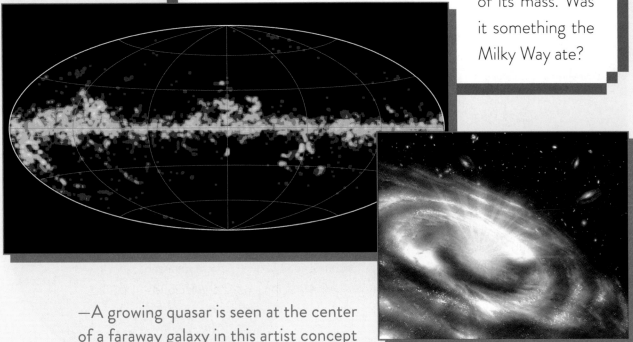

—A growing quasar is seen at the center
of a faraway galaxy in this artist concept

Some hot subdwarfs go a different route. One shifty star was found in 2010 to hold large patches of zirconium, an element used on Earth to make fake diamonds. Keep an eye on that one.

No Warming, No Cry

Without sunlight, starlight, or even a night-light to keep them warm, you'd expect rogue planets to be cold, lifeless rocks. But that might not always be the case. Scientists have theorized that rocky planets with molten cores, like the Earth, may generate enough heat to have water in liquid form, especially if those planets have atmospheres to trap heat. Likewise, huge hot gas giants may be nearly as toasty in interstellar space as they are in nice, snug orbits around a star.

—This artist's conception illustrates a Jupiter-like exoplanet alone in the dark of space, floating freely without a parent star

As the runts of the galaxy, you might expect planets to behave themselves. But no. Some planets aren't content to twirl peacefully around their stars. Instead, these planets go rogue, flung from their orbits by shifts in gravity to wander through space, lonely worlds without a star to call home. How many rogues are there in the Milky Way? About 100 billion. Better lock your doors.

Some of the galaxy's strangest matter isn't matter—it's *antimatter*. Antimatter looks like "regular" matter, but in a Bizarro World twist, antimatter particles have opposite electrical charges and other properties. When matter and antimatter meet, they cancel out—explosively. Particles of matter and corresponding antiparticles annihilate each other in a shower of energy.

There's much, much more matter than antimatter in the universe—thank our lucky non-antimatter stars—but we do know of a huge, lopsided cloud of antimatter 10,000 light-years across. The cloud spits out high-energy gamma rays as matter crosses its path and runs into antimatter particles. And where does it live? Right in the center of our own Milky Way.

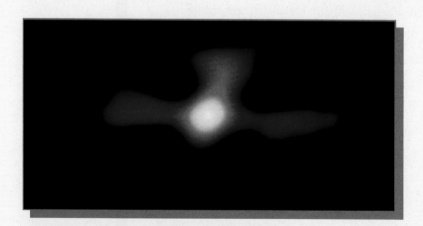

—The antimatter "cloud" at the center of the Milky Way. The bright center is the nucleus of the galaxy; the horizontal structure lies along the plane of the galaxy; and the antimatter "cloud" is located above the bright galactic center.

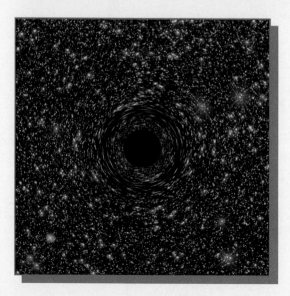

Scientists don't know where this antimatter glob came from. Recent data suggest that dark matter—another not-quite-matter mystery—isn't involved, but other exotic things nearby could be. Pulsars, black holes, X-ray binaries—or a combination of oddities. In the Milky Way, most weird stuff is produced by something else just as weird. That's just how the galaxy rolls.

—How a black hole is theorized to look

IS THAT A REAL THING?
Astrology

Since ancient times, people have used the stars to navigate and to track the seasons. The first calendars, compasses, and GPSes were just people watching the motions of stars.

But not all skywatchers were so practical. Shapes among the stars reminded people of animals and figures from legends. No one knew what the stars, galaxies, and planets really were, so people made up stories to explain what they saw—and what the lights above might mean.

Thus, astrology was created—by ancient peoples imagining how constellations and planets affected them, without knowing those objects are incredibly distant, spinning through cold space, and fully unconcerned about our lives (and birthdays). Thanks to modern astronomy, we know that astrology's claim of distant objects influencing our lives is just superstition. Still, some traits linked by astrologers to particular constellations or zodiac signs really are more common in people born in certain months. But if the fault's not in the stars, where is it?

Turns out, the reason's in the seasons. Studies have shown that people are more likely to develop certain traits—including eating habits, sleep disorders, even long lifespans—depending on the season when they were born. Because constellations also move with the seasons, astrologers may have picked up on some interesting sociological trends. They just whiffed when they associated those trends with the stars, and not the calendar. Total Virgo move, there.

—FROM PAGE 139 . . .

Bizarre Space Trivia, Answer

Voyager 1, launched in 1977, has escaped the solar system, traveling around 38,000 miles per hour. At that rate, how long would it take Voyager 1 to reach the Milky Way's center?

a. 450 years

b. 450,000 years

c. **450,000,000 years** (correct)

—Voyager 1

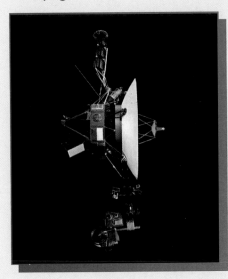

The Details: NASA's plucky Voyager 1 probe has gone where no man—or woman, kid, or craft—has gone before: outside the solar system. In 2017, Voyager 1 was 13 billion miles away from the sun, nearly 140 times farther away than Earth! But that's just peanuts to galactic distances.

We're sitting about halfway out a Milky Way arm, 26,000 light-years from the center. By comparison, Voyager 1 has traveled not quite a "light day" from the sun. That's one day out of 26,000 years, at nowhere near light speed. We hope Voyager packed plenty of comics to read.

SECTION 6
Your Universe and You

If the Milky Way's size makes Earth look like a speck of dust, the universe makes our galaxy look like an even dinkier dust speck. And the universe has filled all that space with some pretty crazy stuff. From billions of galaxies to X-ray stars, black holes, and things we don't even have names for yet, there are more things in the heavens than are dreamt of in our philosophy.

Bizarre Space Trivia

We know that the Earth is round, space is curved, and the Milky Way is shaped like a spiral. But what shape is the universe?

a. A sphere, expanding from the center

b. A saddle, curving outward on the edges

c. A flat sheet, with no curves at all

— Find out the answer at the end of the section (p. 203)! —

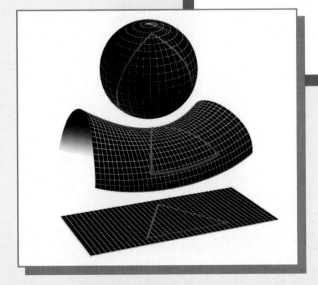

—The three possible explanations of the shape of the universe

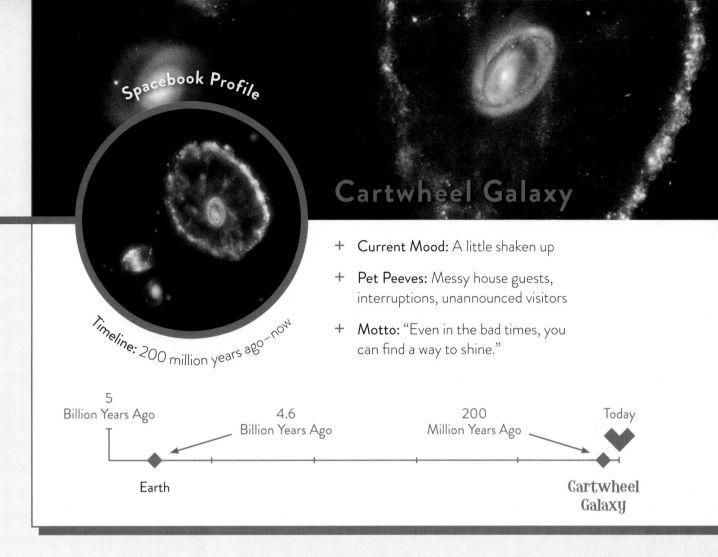

Cartwheel Galaxy

+ **Current Mood:** A little shaken up

+ **Pet Peeves:** Messy house guests, interruptions, unannounced visitors

+ **Motto:** "Even in the bad times, you can find a way to shine."

Timeline: 200 million years ago–now

| 5 Billion Years Ago | 4.6 Billion Years Ago | 200 Million Years Ago | Today |

Earth

Cartwheel Galaxy

THE GALAXY MENAGERIE

The size of space—its mind-numbing *bigness*—comes at you in waves. Or in layers, like an onion—only instead of ever-smaller layers hidden underneath, space has always-bigger layers above you, every time you peel another away. Just when you picture how far it is to the moon, you learn how much farther away the sun is. And then how way, way out there the outer planets are. And how much wider the solar system stretches, after those. And then about the billions of other stars and solar systems dotting the Milky Way like popcorn on a galactic Christmas tree.

Every time you turn around, it seems that distance figures in space have another zero or three tacked on. But once you reach galaxy size, that's finally the end, right? Nope. It's barely even the beginning. (And you thought peeling onions made people cry.)

Our galaxy is an impressive cosmic sculpture, a swirling platter of matter 100,000 light-years across. But just like our sun is a typical, garden-variety example of the Milky Way's 200 billion or so stars, the Milky Way itself is just another galaxy among others. Many, many others—recent findings suggest there are around 2 trillion galaxies in the observable universe. In other words, for every one of the myriad uncountable stars in our galaxy, there are 10 galaxies out there, each with billions of stars of their own. That's space for you; it'll get you every time.

Do You See What I (Fore)See?

The estimate of 2 trillion galaxies was made in 2016 and is roughly 10 times larger than previous estimates of the number of observable galaxies. The new research used existing observations but added mathematical models, which predicted the presence of many very old galaxies too faint to see with current telescopes. The estimate may be confirmed when NASA's James Webb Space Telescope, capable of viewing these faint ancient galaxies, launches in 2018.

—James Webb Space Telescope

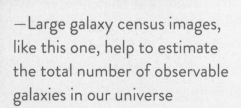

—Large galaxy census images, like this one, help to estimate the total number of observable galaxies in our universe

Sagittarius A*

+ **Hobbies:** Personal growth, gaining mass, bulking up

+ **Recent Trips:** I don't go to places—places come to me.

+ **Quote:** "Black is the new black."

Timeline: 13 billion years ago–now

| 14 Billion Years Ago | 13 Billion Years Ago | Today |

Birth of the Universe   Sagittarius A*

NONE MORE BLACK

They say too much of a good thing can be dangerous. That's true whether you're filling water balloons or touring the Wonka factory, and it's also true when it comes to gravity.

Sure, the Earth's gravity is great—it keeps us from flying off in wild directions or losing our keys in outer space. (It also keeps some of us from dunking a basketball, but that's another story.) We feel gravity because the Earth has mass. All objects with mass have a gravitational pull, but you don't feel it from most things—like a desk or your grandfather—because they're not much more massive than you (even if Granddad's been into the Wonka chocolates again).

181

The Earth is vastly more massive than we are, though, so we feel its gravity. And the Earth and other planets feel the gravity of the much larger sun, which keeps them in orbit and not whizzing off into interstellar space. So far, so good! But what if an object were so massive and dense that nothing nearby could escape its pull? Not planets, not stars, not even waves of light?

That object would be a *black hole*, predicted to exist about a hundred years ago from the work of physicist Albert Einstein. Although Einstein argued that black holes wouldn't actually form in reality, evidence for them was discovered in 1971. And now, we find them everywhere.

A Whole Lotta Holes

When we say black holes are everywhere, we mean it. In the Milky Way alone, scientists estimate there are several hundred million black holes lurking among the stars, each with around 3–30 times the sun's mass packed into a ball a few dozen miles across. Because black holes trap light and energy, they can't be detected directly. Scientists have located black holes in our galaxy by finding X-rays and other signals from stars and heated gas being pulled into the black holes.

—The blue dots show galaxies that contain supermassive black holes emitting high-energy X-rays

—A spectrum of a black hole, with the highest-energy X-rays near the center and the lower-energy X-rays farther out

—Colliding galaxies whose central black holes (revealed in spectroscopic pink light) are merging

How Does Your Black Hole Grow?

It's not known how supermassive black holes form. They may be the shells of gigantic stars formed in the early universe, or the results of mergers of smaller black holes. Or both, or something else entirely. Stellar black holes do appear to merge, though. Although the largest detected has a mass around 30 times the sun's, recent data suggest the presence of "intermediate-mass" black holes of hundreds to thousands of solar masses. Not supermassive—but massive-er.

Most, perhaps all, black holes form from the remains of dying stars. When a massive star runs out of fuel, it sneezes away its outer layers in a supernova explosion. The leftovers collapse into a white dwarf or neutron star—but it doesn't always stop there. If the stellar remnants are at least 3–4 times more massive than the sun, then no known force can stop them from shrinking into a black hole.

Stellar black holes are common in the universe, but they're small gravitational potatoes compared to their supermassive black hole cousins. These black holes can be around the size of the sun, but with millions to billions of times more mass. Supermassive black holes sit in the center of most galaxies, growing ever larger as they pull in stars, gas, and most everything else.

Black holes in galactic centers can produce the most dramatic spectacles in the universe when they become *active galactic nuclei*. Matter falling into a supermassive black hole forms a disc around the black hole. The material heats up as it spirals and gravity pulls it toward the black hole, releasing bursts of radiation. This radiation often outshines the billions of stars in the galaxy put together, and can include visible light, ultraviolet, radio, X-ray, gamma, or cosmic rays.

Active galactic nuclei come in several flavors, based on the radiation they emit. Quasars, blazars, radio galaxies, and Seyfert galaxies are a few types—some of which shoot twin jets of radiation from their galactic cores. But all active galactic nuclei produce enormous energy; for quasars, the most powerful

A Hole of Our Very Own

Most galaxies house a central black hole, and the Milky Way is no exception. Our local supermassive neighbor is Sagittarius A* (pronounced "a-star") and is not currently an active galactic nucleus—but not long ago (in cosmic terms), it may have been. Scientists have found evidence that 2 million years ago, Sagittarius A* emitted much more radiation, and may have been 10 million times brighter than it is today. We would definitely call that "active"!

—How a quasar is theorized to look

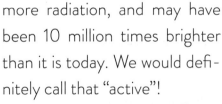

—How a "feeding" black hole, digesting remnants of a star, is theorized to look

category, up to a trillion times our sun's energy, or 100 times more than the entire Milky Way!

No one knows what the inside—or outside—of a black hole is like. Everything we detect, including a finding of a black hole "feeding" on a doomed star for 10 years, comes from material falling toward the black holes, not the black holes themselves. Physics theories give us some ideas about black holes' structure—but those ideas can be pretty strange and don't always agree.

Scientists think the center of a black hole is a tiny point called a *gravitational singularity*, which contains the black hole's entire mass. At some distance surrounding the singularity is the *event horizon*, from inside which no object, energy, or even light can escape. Physicists long believed that event horizons are invisible boundaries; if you passed through one, you wouldn't know that you could no longer escape the black hole's gravity—although it would stretch you out as you fell closer, in a process called *spaghettification*. (Honestly. We didn't make that up.)

But in 2012, scientists used ideas from quantum physics to suggest that event horizons are literal "firewalls"—bubbles of boiling particles that burn anything passing through them to a crisp. So, hardly "invisible." The debate about event horizons also affects whether information is lost in black holes and whether they can evaporate over time. So far, no one knows for sure.

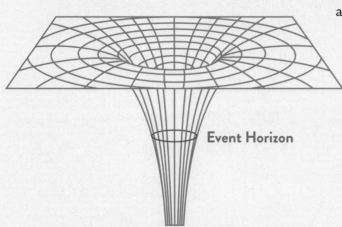

Event Horizon

Gravitational Singularity

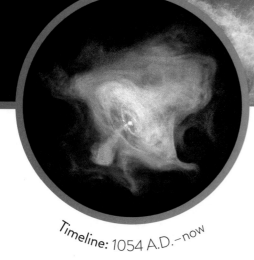

Crab Pulsar

+ **Current Mood:** Getting dizzy

+ **Favorite Workout:** Spin class!

+ **Pet Peeve:** Feeling like I'm constantly running in circles

Timeline: 1054 A.D.–now

| 1000 A.D. | 1054 A.D. | 1572 A.D. | | Today |

Crab Pulsar

Tycho's Supernova

A QUIRKY, KOOKY COSMOS

With so much of the universe undetected and so many cosmic oddballs already mentioned, you might expect the rest of the observable universe to behave itself, right? Nope.

Consider, for instance, fast radio bursts, or FRBs. These high-energy radio wave pulses last only a few milliseconds, but have been detected around 20 times so far by radio telescopes. The FRBs blast from regions of space billions of light-years away—one even seems to repeat!—and no one knows for sure what causes them. FRBs may come from exotic stars or black holes, but the search for answers is ongoing.

Radio's One-Hit Wonder

Not all RBs are F. That is, some cosmic radio bursts last more than a fraction of a second—or at least, one did. In 1977, Ohio State University's "Big Ear" radio telescope detected a massive radio signal over a minute long. Dubbed the "Wow! signal" because the scientist reviewing the data readout circled the signal and wrote "Wow!" in the margin, the mysterious finding became famous. In 2017, the signal was linked to emissions from a passing comet.

—A scan of the original printout with Jerry R. Ehman's handwritten exclamation

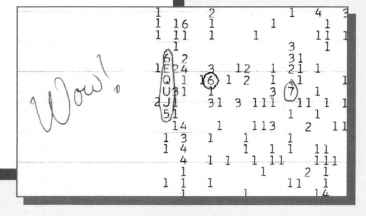

Some cosmic phenomena aren't so mysterious—at first. Take cosmic rays, which are poorly named—they're actually particles—but fairly well understood. Most cosmic rays are stripped-down atomic nuclei, usually hydrogen or helium. The Earth's atmosphere is bathed constantly in cosmic rays, which come from the sun, supernova explosions, other stars, other galaxies, you name it. Cosmic rays are pretty standard stuff. Until they break the speed limit.

Science says that cosmic rays above a certain energy will interact with the space they travel through, slowing down and reducing their energy. But rarely, astronomers detect a ray that doesn't follow the rules; some have been seen with energies more than 5 times over the theoretical limit. If these rays haven't been slowed down yet, it suggests they were spewed out from something very close by—and very powerful. But what? So far, we can only guess.

Fly Away, Ray

One of the most energetic cosmic rays ever detected was the "Oh-My-God" particle seen by Utah's "Fly's Eye" array in 1991. That ray's energy was about the same as a thrown baseball or a dropped bowling ball. But instead of the energy being spread across countless atoms in a ball, it was all in one particle, zooming at 99.99% the speed of light!

A black hole might be a star's strangest swan song—but there are other odd ways to go. Among neutron stars—incredibly dense stellar cores surviving their stars' supernovae, but not quite massive enough to form black holes—a certain exotic flavor stands out: *pulsars*.

Pulsars are so named because they "pulse" incredible bursts of radiation in cycles of a few seconds or less. The radiation shoots out in a steady beam of energy aligned with the neutron star's massive magnetic field—many millions of times stronger than Earth's. Because the star rotates, and its magnetic field also spins out of sync, the beam is twirled around with every rotation, often at millisecond speeds. Pulsars are basically hyperactive cosmic lighthouses.

Pulsar radiation can be anywhere on the electromagnetic spectrum. The Crab Pulsar, for example, formed after a supernova blast seen in 1054 A.D. This pulsar spins 30 times a second, with each spin shooting radiation—from gamma rays, to visible light, to X-rays—toward the Earth.

Although more than 2,000 pulsars have been found in the Milky Way, scientists still aren't sure what makes them tick. Or pulse, or anything else, making pulsars another cosmic mystery.

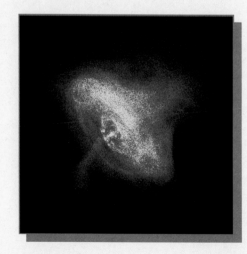

—Jet-like structures produced by high-energy particles blast away from the Crab Pulsar

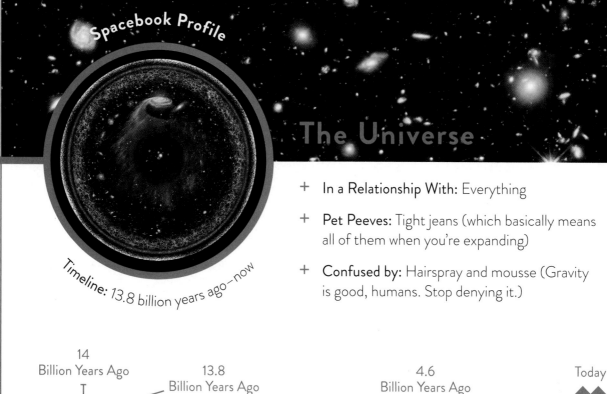

The Universe

+ **In a Relationship With:** Everything

+ **Pet Peeves:** Tight jeans (which basically means all of them when you're expanding)

+ **Confused by:** Hairspray and mousse (Gravity is good, humans. Stop denying it.)

Timeline: 13.8 billion years ago–now

| 14 Billion Years Ago | 13.8 Billion Years Ago | 4.6 Billion Years Ago | Today |

The Universe   **Earth**

CONGRATULATIONS! IT'S A UNIVERSE!

At some point in your life, you have probably stared at the night sky and asked, "How the heck did I get here?"

(You've probably asked the same question in the middle of the school cafeteria, too. We can help you with the "understanding the beginning of the universe" part. Understanding the Chef's Surprise is beyond our scientific jurisdiction.)

The simple answer is that the universe started out extremely small and blew up to the ginormous monstrosity it is today (and it keeps getting ginormous-er). The Big Bang theory is the prevailing scientific principle that describes the history of the universe. (Yep, it was a theory before it was a TV show. The universe did not start with Sheldon Cooper, despite what he may think.)

You are here

—A baby picture of the universe: a full-sky map of the oldest light in the universe, where the colors indicate warmer and cooler spots

When people think of the Big Bang, they often envision a huge explosion, but the "bang" was an expansion of space that started at a small, dense, extremely hot center. Scientists have even found leftover heat caused by the initial Big Bang. This heat—called *cosmic microwave background radiation* (CMB)—is the oldest form of light we know.

Pigeon Poop? Nah, Just the Birth of the Universe

In 1964, astronomers Arno Penzias and Robert Wilson were frustrated. Their telescope seemed to be malfunctioning, because it was making a very unusual sound. They thought the sound was due to pigeon poop on the antenna, but after they cleaned it and got rid of the pigeons, the sound persisted. The malfunction turned out to be the first discovery of cosmic microwave background radiation, which scientists now use to study the Big Bang.

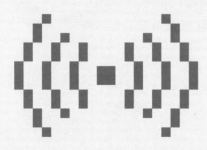

—The Holmdel Horn Antenna on which Penzias and Wilson discovered the cosmic microwave background radiation

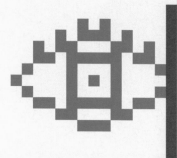

—Chandra X-ray
Observatory

CMB, With Your Glow So Bright . . .

. . . won't you guide NASA's Chandra X-ray Observatory tonight? In February 2016, Chandra tracked CMB radiation to a jet created by a supermassive black hole in a very old area of our universe. The region formed only 2.7 billion years into the universe's life. And the scientists weren't even looking for it! Chandra just happened to detect it when the scientists were working on something else. Thanks for keeping an eye out, Chandra!

—Edwin Hubble

Early space observers thought that the universe was infinite, unchanging, and ageless. They thought the universe was always here, and would always be here in the exact same state. Edwin Hubble (1889–1953) was the first astronomer to offer significant proof that the universe is expanding.

Hubble started his career as a high school basketball coach, but astronomy was always his first passion. He opted to go back to school to study astronomy in 1914. During Hubble's day, most astronomers thought the Milky Way galaxy made up the entire universe. Nebulae were known, but they were thought to be nearby objects made of gas and dust. In October 1923, Hubble proved them all wrong. He found a nebula in the constellation of Andromeda. After analysis, he learned that he was looking at another galaxy! The newspapers went ballistic. *The New York Times* referred to these new galaxies as "island universes."

—To help visualize Hubble's Law, imagine a loaf of raisin bread dough that has been baked in the oven. As the dough doubles in size, so does the space between raisins. Those raisins located farther apart move away from each other more rapidly.

After his amazing discovery, Hubble made another one. In 1929, he learned that most of the galaxies were moving away from each other, which suggested that the universe was expanding. Prior to Hubble, Albert Einstein had theorized the universe was expanding, but Hubble proved Einstein to be correct. The universe was not static, after all. It grows, changes, and expands, a principle now commonly referred to as *Hubble's Law*.

—Georges Lemaître

Father of the Big Bang

Belgian Catholic priest and astronomer Georges Lemaître first published his theory on an expanding universe in 1927, 2 years before Hubble's discovery of expanding galaxies. He made his theory based on the previous work of Einstein and Dutch astronomer Willem de Sitter. After Hubble's finding, Georges Lemaître proposed the theory of the Big Bang in 1931, which scientists still use as their basis for understanding the history of the universe.

After the bang, the universe continued to expand in every direction. It also cooled, allowing subatomic particles to eventually form atoms, the building blocks of matter. These atoms eventually formed clouds of dust. Gravity pulled these dust clouds together, forming planets, moons, and all other objects in our universe. The scientific answer to "How did we get here?" is quite incredible, when you think of where we (meaning everything in the universe) started.

Today, the universe continues to expand. Over time, some of the galaxies we see in our telescopes will not be able to be spotted by those same telescopes, because they will have moved past our range of detection. But how fast is the universe expanding? Astronomers are trying to lock down something called the *Hubble constant*, a mathematical unit that will help them calculate how fast the universe is expanding. In January 2017, the newest measurements for the Hubble constant were revealed based on data collected by space scientists from all over the world. Someday soon, scientists may have a better estimate of the size and age of our mighty universe.

—Cosmic Background Explorer (COBE) satellite

How Do We Know What We Know?

Much of what we know about the beginning of the universe comes from mathematical calculations, computer modeling, and the analysis of CMB radiation. In the 1990s, NASA launched the Cosmic Background Explorer (COBE) satellite to analyze CMB data. The BOOMERanG and WMAP space missions followed suit. The Planck satellite (from the European Space Agency) collected data from 2009 to 2013. Data from this satellite revealed that the universe was slightly older than we thought (by a few hundred thousand years).

Dark Matter

+ **Personality:** Shy and stealthy

+ **Favorite Hobby:** Pranks (I can move things, and you won't even see me!)

+ **Favorite Book Character:** Harry Potter (I dig his invisibility cloak.)

Timeline: ?

? Dark Matter   ? Dark Matter   ? Dark Matter   Today

WHERE NO ONE HAS GONE BEFORE

There is a *lot* we don't know about the universe, mostly because we don't have the capacity to directly observe it. The universe contains stars, planets, moons, galaxies, dust, and gas, but scientists think that this observable matter only makes up about 5% of the entire universe. The other 95% is stuff we can't even see or detect.

Some of this stuff is thought to be dark matter. Dark matter doesn't reflect or absorb light, so scientists cannot see it. But they suspect it's there based on the movement of other objects. Some bodies in space behave as though they have a much larger mass than they do. Other objects move in gravitational patterns that suggest there is some form of unseen matter out there.

The universe contains:

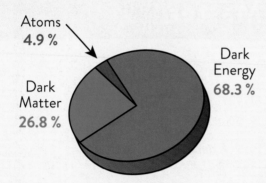

Atoms
4.9 %

Dark
Matter
26.8 %

Dark
Energy
68.3 %

Even more mysterious is dark energy, which may make up most of our universe. In 1998, scientists discovered that our universe was expanding at a faster rate than expected. For this to occur, energy needs to be involved, but (you guessed it) they couldn't detect any. This undetectable energy was named *dark energy*. The idea of dark energy has been debated by scientists. In 2017, a new simulation found that dark energy may not exist. The findings still need further research, but one thing is clear—we're still in the dark about dark energy.

(Special note: Despite astronomers' hobby of putting the word *dark* in front of things they can't observe, this does not work for everything. You can't get out of your math homework by telling your teacher it is "dark algebra.")

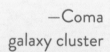

A Glimpse Into the Darkness

In 1933, Fritz Zwicky coined the term *dark matter* when he noticed a puzzling thing about a cluster of galaxies called the *Coma galaxy cluster*. He observed that these galaxies had very fast orbits, but the mass of the galaxies didn't support the gravitational attraction needed for this super-duper spinning. He concluded that there was another form of matter that couldn't be detected to make up for this missing mass.

—Coma
galaxy cluster

Dark Matter Is a WIMP!

All matter is made up of particles. In solids, these particles are packed very closely together. In gases, they are spread farther apart. Because dark matter particles do not seem to interact with known matter very much, scientists call them WIMPs, which stands for Weakly Interacting Massive Particles.

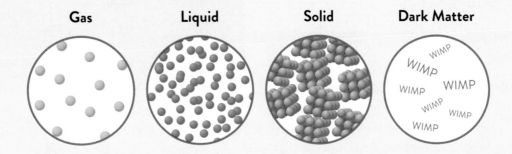

When you look at a bright red apple, your eyes detect light waves that reflect off of it. Your eyes then send a signal to the brain, and the brain processes the color and shape of the apple. Visible light is an electromagnetic wave, and it makes up a very small portion of the electromagnetic spectrum. Many waves we can't see, like infrared rays, microwaves, and X-ray waves, also make up the spectrum (see diagram on p. 7).

We can directly observe things in the universe that interact with light, but there are limitations as to how far into the universe we can see. Light travels extremely fast, but the universe is also massive, so it takes time for light from faraway galaxies to reach us. Simply put, we can only observe light that has had time to get from where it began to where we are in the universe.

—Speed of light

186,282 miles per second or
299,792,458 meters per second

Getting a Better (and Bigger) View

While we wait for light from distant galaxies to reach us, there is *plenty* of stuff in our observable universe to peep at. In late 2016, the Hubble Space Telescope completed a census of the galaxies in our observable universe and found that there are 10 times more galaxies than previously thought. That's a lot of sky peering for us to do!

—Infrared census of the Milky Way

Looking at distant galaxies is like time traveling. When we see them, we're not seeing them as they appear today. We are seeing them as they looked when they first emitted that light. For faraway galaxies, we could be seeing them as they were thousands, millions, or even billions of years ago. Even our own sun is a time traveler. It takes about 8.4 minutes for the sun's light to reach Earth, so the sun you see in the sky right now is really the sun from 8.4 minutes ago!

How Long It Takes Light to Reach Earth

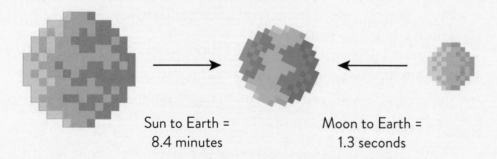

Sun to Earth = 8.4 minutes

Moon to Earth = 1.3 seconds

When you hear about scientists looking at exoplanets and distant galaxies, you might hear them say that they are looking for a planet that could support "life as we know it." The "as we know it" part sounds a bit dramatic, doesn't it? Couldn't we just say we're looking for life, and kill the man-eating alien movie vibe?

When scientists say "life as we know it," they are referring to life in the way we know it on Earth. Scientists do not rule out the possibility of other forms of life, but we don't have any evidence that any other form of life exists. However, we know *we* exist, so planets with Earth-like conditions are the best

places to find "life as we know it." In fact, studying some of our stranger Earth residents might help us to understand how life on other plants could evolve. Extremophiles are organisms that exist in places most living things cannot, including pools of acid, extremely cold or hot environments, or areas without oxygen. Studying these thrill-seeking organisms on Earth might help us detect life on other planets.

—Thermophiles, a type of extremophile that can live at high temperatures, produce some of the bright colors of Grand Prismatic Spring, Yellowstone National Park

How Do We Know What We Know?

We don't! Scientists don't have all of the answers to every question in the universe, but they can make theories and predictions supported by current evidence. Theories evolve as new evidence is discovered, which is part of the fun! In science, the journey to finding the answer to a scientific question is long (and some questions may never be fully answered), so every new discovery is a cause for celebration. Will you be the one who discovers the next big thing in space? Start peeping at the sky and see what you can see!

IS THAT A REAL THING?
Black Hole Sucking Up the Earth

When CERN Labs in Switzerland announced their plans to turn on the Large Hadron Collider (LHC), some people feared it would create a black hole that would "suck up the Earth." This massive particle accelerator has a circumference of 17 miles (27 kilometers)—larger than Manhattan! It's a giant atom-smashing machine, and scientists hope to use it to recreate the conditions from the Big Bang to better understand how our universe formed.

But can this massive machine suck up the Earth? Well, first of all—black holes do not "suck things up" like a vacuum. A perfect vacuum is a space that has no matter, not even air. Black holes are areas with very dense matter, so they are definitely not vacuums.

The LHC can form black holes, but they would be miniscule—too small to power a light bulb, much less swallow the Earth. After rigorous safety tests, the LHC began initial testing in 2009, and it has been running ever since. So, finish that homework already. You're not going to be able to use "the LHC's black hole swallowed my history paper" excuse any time soon.

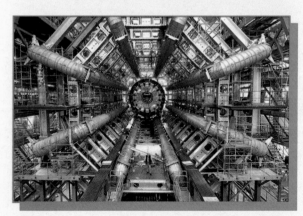

—The Large Hadron Collider

—FROM PAGE 173 . . .

Bizarre Space Trivia, Answer

We know that the Earth is round, space is curved, and the Milky Way is shaped like a spiral. But what shape is the universe?

a. A sphere, expanding from the center

b. A saddle, curving outward on the edges

c. A flat sheet, with no curves at all (correct)

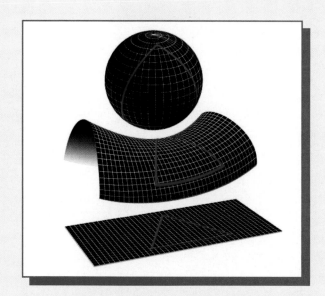

—The three possible explanations of the shape of the universe

The Details: Cosmologists, or scientists studying the nature of the universe, have wondered about its shape for years. As it turns out, the answer has a lot to do with math, specifically geometry.

(Yeah, that scared us, too. But don't worry; you won't need scratch paper. We promise.)

The choices above represent three types of curvature: (1) positive, where points reach toward each other, forming a closed sphere; (2) negative, where points stretch away from each other; and (3) no curving, where points line up in a regular grid. In either sort of curved shape, geometry goes haywire—lines that start out parallel grow closer or spread apart the farther they extend.

By looking at patterns across space, we can see whether things curve together, apart, or not at all. Studies of the cosmic microwave background radiation, seen across all known space, suggest the universe, as far as we can see, is flat. It seems the cosmos is a plain old plane.

BIBLIOGRAPHY

The websites listed below are the most commonly used sources in *Bizarre Space*. For a full list of the references used in each chapter, please visit http://www.prufrock.com/bizarrespace.aspx.

EarthSky
http://earthsky.org

European Space Agency
http://www.esa.int

NASA
https://www.nasa.gov

NASA Goddard Space Flight Center: Imagine the Universe!
https://imagine.gsfc.nasa.gov

NASA Solar System Exploration
https://solarsystem.nasa.gov

NASA Space Place
https://spaceplace.nasa.gov

Sky & Telescope
http://skyandtelescope.com

Smithsonian.com
http://www.smithsonianmag.com

Space.com
https://www.space.com

Universe Today
https://www.universetoday.com

ABOUT THE AUTHORS

Jenn and Charlie are Boston-based science nerds who met through stand-up comedy. By day, Jenn writes science textbooks and Charlie slings data for a cancer research company. By night, they make comedy films and debate whether quarter moons are half light or half dark.

—Jenn Dlugos and Charlie Hatton

IMAGE CREDITS

The publisher would like to thank the following for their permission to reproduce their illustrations:

Abbreviation key: t–top; m–middle; b–bottom; l–left; r–right (m); 80: NASA; 82: WikiCommons/NASA/W. Liller - NSSDC's Photo Gallery (NASA); 83: NASA/JPL-Caltech (t), ESA/Rosetta/MPS for OSIRIS Team MPS/UPD/LAM/IAA/SSO/INTA/UPM/DASP/IDA (m), WikiCommons/ESA/ATG MediaLab (b); 85: NASA/Johns Hopkins University Applied Physics Laboratory/Southwest Research Institute (t), NASA/Johns Hopkins University Applied Physics Laboratory/Southwest Research Institute (m); 86: NASA/Johns Hopkins University Applied Physics Laboratory/Southwest Research Institute; 87: NASA/Johns Hopkins University Applied Physics Laboratory/Southwest Research Institute; 88: Wikipedia/A. Feild (Space Telescope Science Institute) (l), Wikipedia/NASA/ESA (r); 89: NASA/JPL-Caltech/UCLA/MPS/DLR/IDA (t), NASA/JPL-Caltech/UCLA/MPS/DLR/IDA (m); 92: NASA/JPL-Caltech; 93: WikiCommons/NASA (t), Wikipedia/NASA/JPL-Caltech/R. Hurt (SSC-Caltech) (b); 94: Wikipedia/NASA, ESA, and M. Brown; 95: NASA/JPL-Caltech; 97: NASA (t), WikiCommons/PD-NASA (m); 98: NASA/SDO/AIA; 99: NASA/GSFC/Solar Dynamics Observatory; 100: NASA/Goddard Space Flight Center; 101: NASA/JPL-Caltech; 102: Wikipedia/ESO/Tomruen, nagualdesign; 103: NASA/JPL-Caltech/UCLA/MPS/DLR/IDA; 107: Wikipedia/NASA/ESA/Hubble Heritage Team (STScI/AURA)/ESA Hubble Collaboration-HubbleSite (t), WikiCommons/NASA/ESA/J. Muzerolle (STScI)/E. Furlan (NOAO and Caltech)/K. Flaherty (University of Arizona/Steward Observatory)/Z. Balog (Max Planck Institute for Astronomy)/R. Gutermuth (University of Massachusetts, Amherst) (m); 108: NASA/JPL-Caltech/University of Wisconsin; 109: NASA/JPL-Caltech/Calar Alto Obsv./Caltech Sub. Obsv.; 110: NASA; 111: NASA/JPL-Caltech/Harvard-Smithsonian CfA; 113: Robert Gendler (m); 115: Wikipedia/*New York World-Telegram and the Sun Newspaper*; 116: NASA (t), NASA (m); 119: NASA/JPL-Caltech/UCLA (t), MPIA/NASA/Calar Alto Observatory (m); 120: Wikipedia/Margarita Karovska (Harvard-Smithsonian Center for Astrophysics)/NASA; 122: NASA; 123: NASA/JPL-Caltech (t), NASA/JPL-Caltech/STScI/CXC/SAO (m), NASA/JPL-Caltech/UCLA (b); 125: NASA/JPL-Caltech/GSFC (t), ESA/NASA/SOHO (m); 126: NASA (b); 127: NASA/GSFC/Solar Dynamics Observatory (t); 128: NASA/Goddard//SDO (l), NASA (r); 129: NASA/GSFC/Solar Dynamics Observatory; 131: Akira Fujii, European Space Agency (t), WikiCommons/NASA/ESA/H. Bond (STScI)/M. Barstow (University of Leicester) (m); 132: Judy Schmidt (l); 135: ALMA (ESO/NAOJ/NRAO)/E. O'Gorman/P. Kervella; 139: WikiCommons/PD-NASA; 141: NASA/JPL-Caltech (t), ESO/B. Tafreshi (m); 142: NASA/ESA/Martino Romaniello European Southern Observatory, Germany; 143: R. Wesson/ESO; 144: NASA/JPL-Caltech; 145: ESA/Herschel/PACS/SPIRE/J. Fritz, U. Gent; X-ray: ESA/XMM Newton/EPIC/W. Pietsch, MPE; 147: NASA/JPL-Caltech (t), NASA/JPL-Caltech (m); 148: NASA/JPL-Caltech (t), NASA/Goddard Space Flight Center (m), NASA (b); 149: NASA/JPL-Caltech; 150: Wikipedia/Diceman Stephen West (l), Wikipedia/Dr. Schorsch (r); 151: NASA/JPL/Caltech/Harvard-Smithsonian Center for Astrophysics; 153: Wikipedia/ESA/Hubble (t), WikiCommons/NASA, ESA/Hubble Heritage Team (STScI/AURA) (m); 154: WikiCommons/Judy Schmidt (t), WikiCommons/NASA/ESA/Evercat (m); 155: WikiCommons/NASA/ESA/M. Robberto (Space Telescope Science Institute/ESA)/Hubble Space Telescope Orion Treasury Project Team (t), WikiCommons/ESO (b); 156: WikiCommons/ESA/NASA; 157: NASA (t), NASA/ESA/JPL/Arizona State University (l), Wikipedia/William Parsons, 3rd Earl of Rosse (r); 159: NASA/JPL-Caltech (b); 160: Wikipedia/NASA/Marie-Eve Naud et al, Gemini Observatory; 161: WikiCommons/NASA/JPL-Caltech (t), NASA/JPL-Caltech (m); 162: NASA/JPL-Caltech; 163: NASA/JPL-Caltech; 166: NASA/Goddard Space Flight Center; 167: ESA/NASA/JPL-Caltech